The Clarity Series

Creating
Passionate Learners

The Clarity Series

We face a challenging paradox. Although education is what people and societies have always turned to as a path to a desirable future, the current systems and structures in place actually stand in the way of achieving that preferred state, hindering the true results needed. In this context, educators and students alike are rapidly becoming casualties of an outdated system of education. Given this context, the education community desperately needs an agenda of hope and a *clarity of vision*. Educators feel ongoing tension between what is and what could be in their profession. Many well intended reformers are, in reality, only adding to the initiative fatigue currently plaguing educators. Often educators are finding themselves stuck somewhere between feeling frustrated and being in a state of perpetual paralysis. Sadly, too many educators wonder, in this dynamic landscape, if they really *can* make a difference.

We believe that educators truly can make a difference. Our author team is passionate about leading change, and we have field tested the processes, practices, and innovations that form the basis of the series. Through these volumes, we intend to equip educational leaders with the vision, mindset, skills, and passion for what is possible in public education's future. We will create a new culture where the best and brightest still want to call this profession their own.

Community-Based Learning:
Awakening the Mission of Public Schools

Holly A. Prast and Donald J. Viegut

Creating Passionate Learners:
Engaging Today's Students for Tomorrow's World

Kim Brown, Tony Frontier, and Donald J. Viegut

The Clarity Series

Creating Passionate Learners

Engaging Today's Students for Tomorrow's World

Kim Brown

Tony Frontier

Donald J. Viegut

Foreword by
Dr. Russell J. Quaglia

CORWIN
A SAGE Company

FOR INFORMATION:

Corwin
A SAGE Company
2455 Teller Road
Thousand Oaks, California 91320
(800) 233-9936
www.corwin.com

SAGE Publications Ltd.
1 Oliver's Yard
55 City Road
London EC1Y 1SP
United Kingdom

SAGE Publications India Pvt. Ltd.
B 1/I 1 Mohan Cooperative Industrial Area
Mathura Road, New Delhi 110 044
India

SAGE Publications Asia-Pacific Pte. Ltd.
3 Church Street
#10-04 Samsung Hub
Singapore 049483

Acquisitions Editor: Dan Alpert
Senior Associate Editor: Kimberly Greenberg
Editorial Assistant: Cesar Reyes
Production Editor: Veronica Stapleton Hooper
Copy Editor: Pam Schroeder
Typesetter: C&M Digitals (P) Ltd.
Proofreader: Dennis W. Webb
Indexer: Marilyn Augst
Cover Designer: Janet Kiesel
Marketing Manager: Amy Vader

Printed in the United States of America

ISBN 978-1-4833-4448-5

This book is printed on acid-free paper.

15 16 17 18 19 10 9 8 7 6 5 4 3 2 1

Contents

Foreword

Our education system is being driven by common practices rather than common sense. Practices such as strict schedules maintained by archaic bell systems and an overabundance of standardized tests, too often decided upon by individuals who have not worked alongside students in years, can be restrictive. The result is a hindrance of what naturally promotes passionate learning—a culture driven by trust, responsibility, and relationships; a positive attitude toward oneself and others; genuine collaboration with a purpose; and meaningful engagement. These are the cornerstones of passion for endeavors in real life, outside the classroom. Isn't that what we are preparing students for? What happens inside the classroom should emulate learning as it occurs in real life. Anything short of that makes *no* sense.

Creating Passionate Learners makes perfect sense. Authors Brown, Frontier and Viegut proficiently pull together the most influential engagement research as well as proven practices and share it in a manner that is readily applicable to teachers and school leaders. As someone who wholeheartedly believes in and promotes the importance of student voice, I must acknowledge my bias (albeit a healthy one!) when saying that the authors are to be commended for consistently looking at learning through the eyes of students. They recognize that students are not only important contributors to improving education, they are indeed the reason for improvement.

Brown, Frontier, and Viegut recognize the importance of ensuring that students are more than heard—students must be an integral, central part of the school improvement process. Throughout the book, they honor students as active participants in this endeavor. It is more than a symbolic role; students should have a genuine voice in schools, with a meaningful purpose. Research conducted by the Quaglia Institute for Student Aspirations has found that when students have a voice, they are seven times more likely to be academically motivated. When students are motivated to learn, they become meaningfully engaged in their learning.

What is meaningful engagement? The answer is complex, yet the authors have tackled it by culling the rich bank of information in the field, ultimately developing the Framework for Creating Passionate Learners. At the core of this framework are *beliefs* that are determined by four prompts: the Growth Mindset ("I Am"); Internal Dialogue ("I Think"); Self-Determination ("I Will"); and Culture ("We Are"). The authors not only effectively achieved the herculean task of synthesizing the information, but they also communicate it in a way that is immediately digestible and applicable. The integration of anecdotes with practical suggestions ensures that teachers and school leaders can immediately address these four factors in their schools.

The need to address engagement is immediate. As I read *Creating Passionate Learners,* I reflected on my own work in education and considered how the lack of student engagement contributes to a participation gap—a gap of the mind, heart, and soul of the learner. How does one fill this gap? To be engaged and participate, students must experience fun and excitement in their learning environment. They should be so involved in their own learning that they lose track of time and space altogether, wondering how the class flew by so quickly. Students should be curious and creative, asking "Why?" or "Why not?" about the world around them, and then actively seeking the answers. Engaged students have a spirit of adventure; they are not afraid to try new things, regardless of whether they may succeed or fail.

With engagement, learning—and therefore participation in learning—becomes important in and of itself. The Quaglia Institute's research has found that when students are deeply involved in the learning process, as characterized by enthusiasm, a desire to learn new things, and a willingness to take positive, healthy steps toward the future, they are *seventeen* times more likely to be academically motivated.

Creating Passionate Learners places students right where they should be—in the midst of it all, in the driver's seat of their own engagement, learning, and motivation. By honoring students as partners in the learning process and listening to student voice, Brown, Frontier, and Viegut challenge readers to work *with* students to increase engagement and ultimately erase the participation gap.

The ideas in *Creating Passionate Learners* underscore the importance of student-centered leadership in improving engagement. When schools recognize the critical importance of student voice and put into practice the Framework for Creating Passionate Learners, students will be more likely to have high aspirations. Students with high aspirations show marked improvements in academic achievement, social awareness, and positive contributions to their school community. When all students believe in themselves, are engaged in their learning, and understand that what they learn today influences who they will become tomorrow—only then will the larger goal of helping students reach their fullest potential be met. Education must be about more than preparing for tests. It must prepare students to be passionate learners for life. It just makes sense.

I offer great appreciation to authors Brown, Frontier, and Viegut for enhancing the understanding of student engagement and its importance in education. *Creating Passionate Learners* is a resource that will help drive change.

Dr. Russell J. Quaglia @DrRussQ

Executive Director and Founder,
Quaglia Institute for Student Aspirations

Author of *Student Voice: The Instrument
of Change* and the *Quaglia School Voice*
suite of survey tools, published by Corwin

Preface

Students' learning journeys can be ordinary—or extra-ordinary—depending on how engaged they are in their education. Learners who leave their current thinking to explore new approaches experience trials and challenge themselves despite fearing the outcome and so ultimately emerge with greater wisdom.

Like Harry Potter, J. K. Rowling's fictional hero who faced battles both internal and external to learn about his own gifts and grow ever stronger, we as learners take a hero's journey by "listening for the call to adventure, accepting the challenge, conquering our fear and claiming the treasure we seek" (Winkler, 2013).

The treasure here is for you, the reader, to embark on the journey to understand how to help students become passionate learners. By picking up this book, you are seeking out your own call for adventure. You'll discover why student engagement should be at the heart of our efforts to improve teaching and learning and how engagement is a defining factor for student success. You'll embark on a mission to reverse the human tragedy of under-engaged students by developing a metric focused on student engagement.

You'll study a framework that connects awareness and understanding of teacher feedback and student mindset, achievement, and passion that can lead to improved professional practice and, ultimately, increases in student achievement. You'll learn how to put student achievement at the forefront of the professional growth and development conversation.

Use this book for professional growth and development and to find tangible engagement strategies and key phrases and questions to work with students toward true engagement and a growth mindset. Follow the examples of engagement at the heart of school improvement planning scattered throughout the book to understand the difference student engagement makes for families, educators, and most importantly, the students we serve.

ABOUT THE BOOK

The first six chapters demonstrate the framework for creating passionate learners. The last two chapters discuss high-leverage reform and how leaders support the framework for creating passionate learners.

Chapter 1 builds the argument for a focus on student engagement through a historical perspective. An alternative approach to thinking about teaching and learning will be explored, leading to next practices in the 21st century.

Chapter 2 helps develop educators' understanding of cognitive, behavioral, and emotional engagement and learn how to create a culture of engagement that emphasizes assessment literacy in every classrooms, building, and the district.

In Chapter 3, readers can explore the power of mindset and understand how a teacher's focus on student effort can change mindset, resulting in a renewed sense of what a child can accomplish. The classroom environment teachers create can increase students' aversion to risk and stifle growth and engagement or increase risk taking and promote growth and engagement.

Chapter 4 shows how intentional language helps develop students' internal dialogue and how teachers' word choice aids students' reflection. Teachers' positive suppositions influence students' views of themselves and translate into student confidence in their classrooms.

Chapter 5 explains the importance of self-determination and the research that benefits students when they perceive their teachers to be autonomy supportive.

Chapter 6 discusses how to set the culture and tone for engagement by defining and recognizing what it looks like and understanding the factors that dampen students' passion for learning.

Chapter 7 highlights how the Framework for Creating Passionate Learners can be used as the filter for high-leverage reform.

Chapter 8 helps building and district leaders understand how to plan and develop transformational change, leading to creating passionate learners.

The Framework for Creating Passionate Learners speaks to the book as a whole and why each chapter is part of the book. It now is up to you to take on the challenge to internalize the substance of the book to engage your students fully so that they can fully reach their potential.

Acknowledgments

Dan Alpert—Thank you for believing in this series and understanding the importance of student engagement.

Nate Breitholt—Your background in graphic design and art are so appreciated. Thank you for sharing your talents with us.

Vibe 22—You have been a second family to me. I am thankful for our journey together.

Coach Hoxtell—My life's lessons were learned through your coaching. Thank you for your sacrifices to coach so many of us.

Mom, Chuck, and my siblings—Thank you for your encouraging words.

Dr. Tony Frontier—I appreciate your insight and seeing things through different eyes.

Dr. Donald Viegut—Thank you for seeing potential in me. You are a true multiplier!

Dr. Holly Prast—What would I have done without my twin these past few years? You have been my cheerleader, support, and friend.

Ryan and Jack Brown—Thank you for your sacrifices these past few years. I love you both!

Brad Brown—Thank you for getting the kids to all of the soccer practices and tournaments, helping with the housework, and being so patient as I spent the past few years researching and writing. Love you!

Teachers everywhere—Thank you for making a true difference in students' lives. I appreciate the many educators who are linked to, engaged in, and believe in the next generation of work on student engagement.

I appreciate the support of those who worked closely with me—my family, Judy, Josh, Jordon, and Logan, and the other authors in the Clarity Series.

For educators and policy makers who know students in school are so much more than test scores and for my family—Jenny, Hannah, and Sam.

To educators, researchers, and authors
whom we have worked with and learned from.

About the Authors

Kim Brown is a PhD candidate at Cardinal Stritch University with her doctoral dissertation focused on student engagement and autonomy-supportive classrooms. In the past 22 years, she has served as a classroom teacher, building principal, assistant director of special education, and director of early learning and currently serves as the director of learning and communication.

Tony Frontier, PhD, is an assistant professor of doctoral leadership studies and director of teacher education at Cardinal Stritch University. He is coauthor of the ASCD book *Effective Supervision: Supporting the Art and Science of Teaching and Five Levers to Improve Learning* and has been recognized by Marquette University as the College of Education's Outstanding Young Alumnus, by Wisconsin ASCD as the state's Outstanding Young Educator, and by ASCD as an Emerging Leader. He can be reached at acfrontier@stritch.edu.

 **Dr. Donald J. Viegut** has served as a classroom teacher, building principal, director of curriculum, deputy superintendent, and superintendent and currently serves as agency administrator of a regional service delivery agency. Don has served as president of Wisconsin Association for Supervision and Curriculum Development (ASCD) and served on the board of directors for ASCD and as chair of the Board of North Central Technical College. Don also served as the chair of the PK–18 Council for the University of Wisconsin–Steven's Point. Don coauthored *Common Formative Assessments*, a million-dollar Corwin publication, and has presented nationally and networked extensively throughout the world. Don earned his doctorate from Western Michigan University.

CHAPTER 1

An Introduction to Creating Passionate Learners

THE EDUCATIONAL ANACHRONISM

In 1950, nearly 50 percent of American adults smoked cigarettes. By 1970, it had fallen to 38 percent. Today, the number is less than 20 percent. What happened? In 1950, research was published in a prestigious American medical journal (Wynder & Graham, 1950) and a prestigious British medical journal (Doll & Hill, 1950) that raised serious questions about the link between smoking and cancer. By the early 1960s, scientific consensus formed; legislation was passed requiring packages to include warning labels and limiting how cigarettes could be advertised. In 1988, the Federal Aviation Administration banned smoking on airplanes. In 2002, the first state passed legislation that banned smoking in public places. Only recently did one of the nation's top *health-care companies stop selling cigarettes.*

Of course, it is common knowledge today that cigarettes cause cancer, cardiovascular disease, and respiratory disease. But in 1950, it was a *truth* that adults have a right to smoke. It was only with research, perseverance, and time that people were able to let go of a set of habits that were justified through antiquated beliefs, norms, and routines about cigarettes. When the idea that *smoking isn't harmful* was refuted, the argument gave way to this: But adults have a right to make their own choices. When the adults-have-a-right-to-make-their-own-choices argument was refuted by research on the impact of secondhand smoke, it became widely acknowledged that the chasm between research in the public interest about smoking and policy in the public interest about health could no longer stand. The "truths" of past policy and practice lagged 50 years behind the truths of empirical evidence and research.

An anachronism is the placement of an object or behavior that is clearly out of place in modern times. Imagine walking into the offices of a booming Internet start-up and being greeted by a secretary with a typewriter and a rotary phone on her desk: anachronism. She greets you, and if you are a man, she asks if she can take your hat: anachronism. If you are a woman, she asks if you are here to drop off lunch for your husband: anachronism. Today, to see someone smoking on a plane or in a restaurant or in a school would be no less of an anachronism than our out-of-step secretary. Research, beliefs, norms, routines, and policy eventually converged in a manner that makes the idea of smoking in these spaces feel as though they are from a bygone era that is completely out of step with modern times.

We believe that education sits at a similar crossroads. There is a growing chasm between research in the public interest about learners and learning and policy in the public interest about schools and schooling. The truths about the purpose of schooling and the truths about how schools have to operate are rooted in a set of habits that are justified by deeply held beliefs, norms, and routines that served schools in a bygone era. As evidence mounts about the skills and dispositions students will need to be successful learners through the 21st century, many of the policies and practices that guide the efforts of educators and learners through the process of schooling are like ashtrays in armrests: omnipresent but anachronistic.

In this book, *Creating Passionate Learners*, we argue that much of knowledge and many of the skills and dispositions that have been accepted as truths about the purpose of schooling in the last

100 years no longer serve learners' needs in the digital age. We argue that many policies and measures of accountability of schools are not only irrelevant in the 21st century, but they are counter to the public interest. We argue that *what* students learn in school may be less important than helping students understand *how* they will learn when they are not in school. We advocate for systems that focus on building student's engagement rather than coaxing students into compliance. We advocate for curricula that are student centered. We advocate for instructional strategies that support student autonomy.

BEYOND THE NEXT MANDATE

Amid the winds of change that are currently blowing through K–12 education in the United States—new standards, new assessments, new evaluation processes, and new accountability measures—classroom teachers and instructional leaders are suffering from initiative fatigue. Each one of these initiatives seems to require a new set of understandings, skills, and strategies in order to be implemented effectively. Amid this fatigue, many educators are asking the same question: How can we be aware of, let alone effectively implement, all of these new, different sets of expectations?

Far from the shores of the United States, John Hattie of the University of Melbourne, Australia, has been wrestling with an even larger question: What instructional practices have the most profound impact on student learning? In one of the most ambitious educational studies ever completed, Hattie (2009, 2012) went about the process of answering this question. Through a synthesis of meta-analyses, more than 53,000 educational studies with a sample of more than 83 million students were considered. He then rank-ordered the impact of more than 400 different practices. Taking the synthesis a step further, he reached a startling conclusion. There are, he argues, two factors that explain a large portion of the influence that schools have on student learning:

- Learning occurs most effectively when each teacher sees his or her classroom through the eyes of his or her students.
- Learning occurs most effectively when each student sees himself or herself as his or her own best teacher.

The symmetry—and the elegance—of these statements are remarkable. What if Hattie's synthesis provides an answer that transcends our collective fatigue? What if, amid our collective initiative fatigue, we became so focused on the next mandate that we lost sight of students and their learning as the reason for our craft?

While mandates are used to establish the *external* targets to measure *achievement*, it is the *internal*, day-to-day interactions between teachers and students that create a context for *learning*. At the core of the interactions in school and life that result in improved learning is a single concept: engagement. Engaging with others is how we learned to speak, survive, and thrive. When teachers and students are deeply engaged in their work, they both embrace the challenges and opportunities of learning. When teachers and students are disengaged from their work, learning becomes a didactic, transactional chore—if it occurs at all.

For too long, classrooms, schools, districts, states, and the feds have focused on improving education by establishing and tracking goals that are easy to measure rather than those that are most important to measure. It is comforting to believe that we can reduce the cumulative effects of a child's education to an attendance log and a test score. It is harder to monitor and measure the extent that a student is curious, persistent, open-minded, and tenacious. But is it any less important? What if, rather than focusing on test scores as the purpose of school, we strove to achieve a higher calling; what if the goal of school was to create passionate learners?

THE INTENT OF POLICIES AND THE ENSUING DEBATES

The politics of test-score-driven accountability legislation such as No Child Left Behind, incentive grants such as Race to the Top, and initiatives such as the Common Core State Standards have been the subject of discussion and debate in Congress and state legislatures and among school boards around the country. Talk radio, televised pundits, and editorial boards have discussed the opportunities and liabilities associated with these initiatives. No

Child Left Behind *expired in 2007.* Absent meaningful federal legislation, the Department of Education created grant programs to encourage states to move forward with sweeping changes related to standards, assessment, and teacher evaluation.

At the core of the intent of these initiatives are accountability and consistency. Policies and incentives related to consistency are driven by this question: *How can we ensure rigorous criteria for quality across schools, districts, and states?* Policies and incentives related to accountability are driven by this question: *What incentives and consequences will ensure that students, teachers, and schools obtain the desired results?* At the core of the debates around these policies and initiatives are evidence and validity. The first debate is focused on the question: *How can we ensure appropriate evidence is utilized to evaluate teacher and student performance?* The second debate is focused on the question: *Who has the right to determine the validity of content standards and assessments?* These four questions have resulted in a robust national dialogue about states' rights, local control, accountability, privacy, and public- versus private-sector employment. Unfortunately, many of the arguments and claims that have framed this dialogue have fallen squarely along politically partisan lines.

Two components seem to be missing from this discussion. First, there has been little dialogue about the assumptions that underlie the intent of these policies. This is important; if we fail to analyze the assumptions that underlie our beliefs about how systems work, a completely rational policy can be put into place that fails to address the meaningful components of that system. Second, in grand educational policy debates that gravitate toward political interests and partisan ideology, endless print and airtime can be used to talk about adults' interests, adults' needs, and adults' concerns. By failing to analyze assumptions or to ensure the debate transcends partisan bickering, students and their needs have been missed entirely in this debate.

Ultimately, students should derive the greatest benefit from discourse, policy, and practice about improving schools. Yet there is a growing sense that the assumption that test scores can be raised by doling out rewards and sanctions for teachers, schools, and states is not only wrong, but it is harmful for kids. Marc Tucker, president of the National Center for Education and the

Economy (2014), captures this sentiment well in his argument that teachers see beyond test score results to their students as

> people whose potential will forever remain locked inside themselves until they can believe in themselves and their possibilities, people for whom their relationships to other people loom far larger than their obligations to turn in their homework, people whose curiosity and eagerness to prove themselves against the challenges of growing into adults are much more important than their score on a test. (p. 13)

Perhaps systems that strove to help learners find their passions, supported each child's capacity to persevere through challenge, and guided each child's efforts to develop strategies that supported their learning in a variety of contexts would yield more positive, long-term results. But these are skills and conditions that are not emphasized as important inputs or as meaningful outputs on large-scale tests and thus are given less emphasis in dialogue, programs, and policies at the local, regional, and national levels.

ASSUMPTIONS DRIVING THE CURRENT CONTEXT

To understand our current context, it is important to consider where we've been. Many "big ideas" from the end of the 19th and the beginning of the 20th centuries are so ubiquitous in our systems of education that we forget that they are *a way*, and not *the way*, of organizing institutions for teaching and learning. Among the most prominent of these ideas are scientific management, the measurement of intelligence, and behaviorism.

The Influence of the Industrial Revolution and Scientific Management

Industrial growth in the late 1800s gave rise to demographic trends in the United States that resulted in larger, more complex municipalities that required larger, more complex school systems. While the industrial revolution drove this change in the size and complexity of schools and districts, it also had a profound effect on how schools were organized and managed.

In the 19th century, schools emphasized the basics of reading, writing, and arithmetic. Additionally, schools were seen as a means to preserve moral values (Spring, 2011). Students' days included recitation, drills to memorize passages of text or build fluency in mathematical operations, and oral quizzes. Government officials saw the opportunity for schools to help students conform and comply with rules, believing that controlling students' actions would make them more likely, as adults, to obey government laws (Spring, 2011). Students who conformed in school did well. Conversely, students who did not respond well to this system found many doors shut. After the Civil War and through Reconstruction, there was tremendous variability in structure, expectations, and curriculum across the United States. Absent a uniform set of expectations for schooling, professional schools and universities would have no way of identifying which candidates had met their criteria for admissions.

In 1892, a group of 10 men established the uniform system of grade levels, courses, and credits that still guide the structure of most high schools today. Six representatives from higher education, three high school administrators, and a representative from Washington, D.C., responded to calls for more consistency, rigor, and quality in American schools by establishing a 12-grade system consisting of eight elementary grades and four years of high school. The committee established a sequence of math, English, language, and science courses for all students. The amount of seat time required for students to earn a credit that would count toward college admission was established at this time as well. More than 120 years later, the decisions of this *Committee of Ten* continue to frame the structure of schooling in America.

Shortly after the Committee of Ten laid their foundation, Frederick Taylor (1911) published his theories of scientific management. Taylor's work emphasized measurement of efficiency and effectiveness of factory workers as a means to improve production. He argued that, if there were 100 ways to perform a task, some methods would be more efficient than others. By studying the various ways a task such as shoveling coal could be performed, *the one best method* could be determined. The scientific manager's role was to implement and monitor these data-driven approaches to improve organizational quality. Taylor's ideas had a profound impact on American organizations; the ideas resonated with engineers, business owners, *and* educators.

Ellwood Cubberley (1922), who literally wrote the book on American public school administration, led a movement to legitimize a science of education by applying Taylor's theories of management to schools. Cubberley described how Taylor's principles could be used to guide school effectiveness. He unabashedly described the role of schools and factories as analogous stating that "our schools are, in a sense, factories in which the raw products (children) are to be shaped and fashioned into products" (Fine, 1997, p. 338).

The industrial revolution and principles of scientific management created a way of schooling in America that emerged from and is analogous to the innovations of the early 1900s. There is tremendous economic utility in rolling uniform products off of an assembly line in batches. Division of labor, organizational efficiency, standardization, and bells signaling when a shift has ended became the hallmarks of manufacturing and schooling at the dawn of the 20th century.

The Influence of Measurements of Intelligence and Behaviorism

If Taylor's principles of scientific management were to be applied to schools, educators needed an approach to most efficiently elicit and measure the product at the core of schooling: student achievement. Psychologists such as Louis Terman and R.M. Yerkes were up to this task (Gould, 1981). In the early 1900s, a science of educational psychology and measurement of intelligence was also taking shape. These pioneers in the field of psychometrics developed tests that measured a variety of intellectual abilities in an attempt to develop valid, reliable methods to quantify intelligence. Furthermore, these tests were used to determine the individuals who possessed the intellectual capacity to accomplish tasks associated with different roles in military service, identify the most intelligent individuals in society in order to provide opportunities to those individuals to reach their potential, and predict which students would be most successful in various academic programs.

These tests were designed under the assumption that intelligence is a *fixed characteristic.* The premise of intelligence, and the intelligence quotient (IQ), as a fixed entity claimed that individuals were born with a set amount of intellectual capacity and there was little that could be done to change that capacity. One could learn new information and improve mastery of a specific subject, but intelligence itself was stable. These fixed intelligence theorists argued that those with higher IQs would learn faster, and more deeply, than those with lower IQs.

New theories of learning were emerging in the early 1900s as well. Ivan Pavlov and Edward Thorndike argued that learning occurs most efficiently through a process of trial and error that is accelerated or inhibited by the relationship between a stimulus and a response (Gould, 1981). At the core of these behaviorist theories was the premise that, if you want more of something, reward it, and if you want less of something, punish it. The greater the intensity of the satisfaction or discomfort from the response, the more quickly the behavior would be either developed or extinguished. In studies on animals, these theories were roundly supported with empirical research. Using these behaviorist principles, mice could be taught to run through mazes, and rats would learn to pull levers for food. When humans were involved in routine, repetitive tasks—whether in a factory or in a school—their behavior could be shaped by a manipulation of rewards and punishments in a similar manner. The learner doesn't need to understand what he or she is doing nor why he or she is doing it. The only thing that matters is that he or she is trained to accomplish a task.

How Scientific Management and Measurement Influence Our Current Educational Context

Scientific management and behaviorism have had a profound impact on the assumptions that have established the set of conditions that are widely accepted as necessary, central components in the institutionalization of assembly lines and schools.

- Both systems strive for *uniformity.* Everyone follows a specific set of processes in order to ensure the output of uniform products. There is little or no need for individuality or creativity.

- Both systems seek *compliance.* Whether or not individuals are executing a designated process and following the rules is more important than whether or not people understand why they are engaged in a process or why they are doing what they are doing.
- Both systems emphasize a *culture of behaviorism.* A person's purpose for accomplishing any task is determined primarily by the tangible rewards directly associated with completion of that task. If the rewards are not enough incentive to complete the task, the person will be punished.
- Both systems emphasize *productivity.* The quantity of work produced by any one individual—as long as it meets certain standards for quality—is deemed more important than producing less work over a longer period of time even if the work is of greater sophistication or complexity.

The placement of these internal conditions as the premise of an industrialized system at the dawn of the 20th century is rational and justifiable. Uniform productivity on an assembly line requires compliance; there *is* one right way. Behaviorism and its associated rewards and punishments work quite well when individuals are asked to do repetitive, disassociated tasks similar to those on an assembly line. But are these components still relevant as the driving forces in organizations in the 21st century? Should these components continue to be the driving forces *for schools* in today's information and service economy? Should these components continue to be the driving forces for schools as they prepare a generation of learners who will retire sometime around the year 2060?

AN ALTERNATE PREMISE: A HUMANIST APPROACH TO EDUCATION AND COGNITIVIST APPROACHES TO LEARNING

For critics of the industrial model of education, *the school as factory* and the *child as a score* were in direct contrast to their call for approaches to schooling that support each child as an individual with unique learning needs. Educators in support of schools and systems that support each child as an individual are well documented in advance of the push for scientific management and behaviorism that guided decisions about schooling in the United States in the early 1900s.

In his article "Where We Came From: Notes on Supervision in the 1840s," Arthur Blumberg (Blumberg & Blumberg, 1985) discusses some of the extensive field notes written by superintendents in an 1845 document titled the "Annual Report of the Superintendent of Common Schools of the State of New York." Their words include a clear awareness of, and the need to create, classrooms built around learners and learning.

On effective teachers:

> To tell one of the secrets of their success, they endeavor to make the interest of their pupils their interest. (Blumberg & Blumberg, 1985, as cited from original source, 1845, p. 74)

On effective instruction:

> The old and almost useless method of teaching almost everything "by rote," is fast giving way to the inductive and analytical system of instruction. Children are taught that they are intellectual beings, that they are endowed with capacities and powers of the mind. (Blumberg & Blumberg, 1985, as cited in original source, 1845, p. 265)

These statements were made 150 years ago, but they were supplanted by the efficiency of scientific management. They precede John Dewey's arguments for democracy in education by 50 years. They precede the cognitive revolution—whereby psychologists considered the role of an individual's thought processes, language, logic, and deductive reasoning as a set of human functions that transcend behaviorism's explanations of reward or punishment or stimulus and response—by more than 100 years.

John Dewey was one of the most prolific writers and thinkers in the field of education in the early 20th century. In his book *Democracy and Education*, Dewey (1916) argued that democracy, not scientific management, *was* the conceptual underpinning of human progress. Rather than seeing schools as a training ground for efficiency and productivity, Dewey argued that schools were a place where students should practice citizenship and further develop the ideals of democracy. Ideas such as a student-centered education, connecting the classroom to the real world, differentiation based on student learning needs, and integration of content areas were espoused by Dewey as ways of bridging the gap between children's passive roles as students and the active roles they would need to play as citizens.

Democracy and individuality were important values in American society after World War II. Dewey's emphasis on democratic ideals received renewed interest and attention in the field of education. Additionally, new research by individuals such as Jean Piaget (1923, 1947), Jerome Bruner (1960, 1966, 1996), and Noam Chomsky and Carlos Otero (2003) formed the basis of a cognitive revolution in psychology. The cognitivists argued that the individual's role in making meaning was a more powerful force in influencing human motivation than approaches that relied on behavioral manipulation. Democratic and cognitivist ideals were conceptual antidotes to inoculate against the tyranny that led to World War II. The specter of schools built on a premise of blind obedience to authoritarian rewards and punishment or the notion that schools should be built on blind devotion to efficiency over humanity were contrary to what Americans had fought against.

The emphasis on cognition over behaviorism and humanism over authoritarianism was evident in the educational literature at this time. For example, in William Burton, Leo Brueckner, and Arvil Barr's (1955) *Supervision: A Social Process*, they described a new set of premises to guide thought and action in classrooms and schools by stating:

> Our older concepts of human nature and its limitations are giving way to newer knowledge which indicates the possibilities and growth of all individuals. Research in biology, medicine, anthropology, psychiatry, psychology and in education itself open [sic] up new hopes and aspirations in the area of human growth and development. Creativity becomes more important than molding individuals to conformity. The authoritarian and coercive school must give way to a democratic institution that achieves its ends through cooperation and participation of all who are concerned with the growth and development of learners. (pp. v–vi)

This statement is remarkable because it captures the essence of the argument we will build upon in this book. It captures the tension between old premises and assumptions and more contemporary premises and assumptions. Unfortunately, while the argument was made 50 years ago, its potential remains largely unfulfilled.

FROM PAST PRACTICE TO NEXT PRACTICE: NEW ASSUMPTIONS FOR SCHOOLS IN THE 21ST CENTURY

Like the American and British medical journals in the 1950s that described the dangers of smoking well before the act of smoking became an anachronism, the quote from Burton et al. (1955) above captures a set of beliefs about schools and learning that have been—and continue to be—affirmed in research. Unfortunately, many of these older concepts of human nature were so central to the 20th-century frameworks of science and commerce that formed our current conceptualization of schooling in the United States that these anachronistic ideas still permeate the form and function of our schools. There are three central tensions in this quote that lay between the anachronistic beliefs about human nature and capacity at the turn of the turn of the 20th century and the best evidence about those claims today.

Tension 1: Fixed, Single-Dimensional Beliefs About Intelligence Versus Incremental, Multidimensional Beliefs About Intelligence

Anachronism: There is a single, fixed trait called intelligence; some people have it, and some people don't. This older concept of human nature is rooted in pseudoscience and elitist ideology from the 1800s and the early 1900s (Gould, 1981).

Best evidence: Intelligence is multidimensional, and human capacity for intelligence rests on a nearly limitless, resilient, malleable, biological platform (Dickmann & Stanford-Blair, 2009; Gardner, 1983; Sternberg, 2005). Remarkable new skills and understandings can be built by anyone with access to external supports to build new strategies for learning (Duckworth, Peterson, Matthews, & Kelly, 2007; Ericsson, Krampe, & Tesch-Römer, 1993).

Tension 2: Behaviorist Beliefs About Compliance Versus Cognitivist Beliefs About Motivation and Engagement

Anachronism: Human behavior is motivated almost solely by a desire to obtain external rewards and to avoid punishments. Behaviorism is rooted in sound research from the first half of the 20th century (Skinner & Belmont, 1993). However, these findings were most robust when shaping behavioral habits or asking individuals to engage in repetitive tasks that have little intrinsic meaning (Pink, 2009).

Best evidence: If you want more of a behavior, consider the relevance and meaningfulness of that behavior as related to one's physiological, social, emotional, and cognitive needs and interests. Individuals choose to engage in, or avoid, tasks depending on the relevance of the task, their belief that they can be successful in accomplishing the task, their belief that their work is important and of value, and their belief that they will be supported if they are not successful (Ariely, 2013; Bandura, 1995; Dweck, 2000; Pink, 2009).

Tension 3: Controlling Behaviors to Determine Another's Action Versus Autonomy Supportive Behaviors to Guide Individual Growth

Anachronism: If an individual needs to learn, then the learner must depend on the teacher to do so; the teacher must select what will be learned, when it will be learned, how it will be learned, and ultimately assess that individual to render a judgment as to whether or not learning has occurred.

Best evidence: If a teacher wants to motivate individuals to achieve, then allow them the opportunity to exercise autonomy, find their own meaningful reasons to engage in the work they value most, and give them the opportunity to build ownership by determining their pathways toward mastery (Ryan & Deci, 2000).

We believe that the gap between the test-driven and accountability-driven system of schools we have today is a result of the inability to place some of these antiquated beliefs about children and learning in the dustbin. Absent a focus on the best evidence of research on intelligence, motivation, and cognition from the last 65 years, we are doomed to address the same questions about accountability and sanctions that we have in the past and end up back where we started in the first half of the 20th century: schools designed to look like factories and produce students who are prepared to work passively on assembly lines in factories.

We believe a system that consciously tends to the contemporary best evidence to guide efforts to support children and improve learning will focus on four key components.

1. Engage students in a culture of learning that is committed to finding solutions to problems that children see as meaningful and filled with purpose.

2. Engage students in tasks that they are motivated to accomplish because they spark students' curiosities and address their needs to develop and master new, relevant content and skills.

3. Engage students in opportunities to make choices about the work they do in a manner that builds ownership of their own learning and supports their needs for independence and autonomy.

4. Engage students in the habit of productive internal dialogue that is responsive to feedback as a catalyst to develop new skills and strategies that develop their capacity to be effective in any domain they choose.

We believe that a system that utilizes these four components as a catalyst for school reform will not only transcend the rush to gain compliance among today's transactional mandates, but it will support the needs of the passionate learners we aspire to serve.

CHAPTER 2

Committing to Engagement Literacy

There was a young runner who was particularly persistent in her drive to achieve. She enjoyed running, and when she got to high school, she began to think she had potential. However, it was the impact of the coach on this runner that made her and her teammates great.

The coach, who was a teacher at her high school, went out of his way to make each student–athlete feel like an important part of the team. He made it a point to talk to each of the runners throughout the week, not only asking questions but listening to his or her responses. Before and after practice, the coach chatted with the athletes about the need to put forth the right effort to strategize for the next weekend's course. They talked about the importance of eating the right foods. They set goals. They talked about the importance of supporting one another. The coach's expectations were high. His feedback was individualized to each runner's needs: affirmation, observation, challenge, and support.

While these athletes and their coach were data driven—they were as focused on times and splits as any other team—they made more progress throughout the year than any other team in their conference. These athletes were not blindly obedient to their coach. They wanted to be at practice. They wanted to improve. No matter how challenging practice was on a particular day, they felt good about being there. These athletes were invested in the team's goals and the means to obtain them. These athletes were engaged.

The coach created a culture of emotional support for one another: *We are capable of great things.* The coach affirmed each athlete's need for reflection: *I think I am good and can get even better.* The coach developed each athlete's vision of the runner he or she was becoming: *I am capable of working hard to achieve my goals.* The coach empowered each athlete as her own best coach: *I can do this.* These athletes were passionate about running.

TEST SCORES TELL ONLY PART OF THE STORY

The cross-country coach knew that his athlete's times mattered, but they weren't all that mattered. If he only focused on their times, he would mistake outputs for inputs. His work as a coach was not to improve their times; it was to build a system of challenge and support that the athletes wanted to be a part of. If we are concerned about kids and not just their achievement, we need to focus on more than just test scores.

Test scores tell only part of the achievement story. In a synthesis of literature on creating learners completed by the University of Chicago Consortium on Chicago School Research, Camille Farrington and her colleagues (2012) cite a variety of studies showing that grades are better predictors than standardized tests scores of high school performance, college persistence, college grade point average (GPA), college graduation, and even earnings nine years after high school. They argue that grades are a better measure of cognitive components such as perseverance and behavioral components, including effort, that ultimately play an even larger role in determining one's level of success or struggle in school and in life.

Another way to think of this is that test scores measure an outcome that is too far removed from the emotional, behavioral, and cognitive inputs that are a child's schooling experience. Absent measures of student perceptions of their engagement in school, schools and communities often are left with achievement measures like high-stakes accountability tests and dropout rates to make inferences about student engagement, yet these inferences may not be warranted (Willms, 2003). In fact, students can do well on achievement tests, yet report low levels of engagement in school (Frontier, 2007). By focusing too narrowly on the academic outcomes measured by these tests, schools may be ignoring the deeper emotional connections and the reflective cognitive skills that are required for students to be passionate about their schooling experience (Catalano, Haggerty, Oesterle, Flemming, & Hawkins, 2004; Scherer, 2005).

Finally, when we rely solely on test scores to define success, our students can become victims of our own complacency. If test scores are high, everything must be good. Richard Elmore (2006) describes this complacency as an epidemic among thousands of nominally high-performing schools whereby test scores are high, but students are disconnected from each other, disenfranchised by their teachers, and disengaged from their work.

IN SEARCH OF SOMETHING MORE

When your students leave your classroom or school, what do you hope they would say about the experience? We've asked this question of thousands of educators over the years and are amazed at the consistency of responses that we hear. Words like *challenged, supported, interested, hopeful,* and *excited* come up again and again. Phrases such as *they were liked, they use what they learned, they knew I cared, they love the subject I teach,* or *they learned something about themselves* are routinely mentioned. What is even more amazing to us is what isn't mentioned. College entrance tests, state tests, grades, multiple-choice questions, state standards, and almost everything else associated with the inputs of academic achievement and outputs of accountability are never mentioned.

Why is there such a gap between what we talk about giving our students and what we hope our students have when they leave? We believe a key part of the challenge is that we lack a shared language to talk about these critically important, but seemingly intangible, components. We lack a shared language of engagement.

In the anecdote about the cross-country team at the beginning of this chapter, components of engagement were relatively easy to identify; they tried hard, they enjoyed being on the team, and they set goals. However, absent a shared language to discuss how to build and support those engaged beliefs and behaviors, it is difficult to build the next program that elicits similar levels of engagement. *He's just one of those people who was born to coach* or *those girls would run hard for anybody* become the means and the ends to create an engaging environment. It is almost as if being engaging or being engaged are by-products of genetics rather than strategy and effort. Fortunately, there is an emerging body of research that clarifies what engagement is, along with the key components of engagement, and that specific strategies can be utilized—by anyone—to support even higher levels of student engagement.

DEFINING STUDENT ENGAGEMENT

Like the word *intelligence, engagement* has a variety of definitions and measures. Unlike intelligence, there are no prevailing definitions or widely utilized psychometric tools by which to measure the construct (Fredricks, Blumenfeld, & Paris, 2004). The challenge of defining, operationalizing, and measuring engagement is similar to the challenges faced when approaching other broad psychological constructs ranging from happiness to anxiety; the definitions and measures may vary broadly from one study to the next (Elliot & Dweck, 2005).

Engagement is a meta-construct, which simply means it has many different components. When students are engaged, they are attentive; commit time, attention, and effort; and persist with tasks (Schlechty, 2011). Definitions of engagement have included student sense of belonging, participation in classes, and attendance (Willms, 2003); the narrow channel between boredom and anxiety (Csikszentmihaly, 1990); a psychological process of attention, interest, investment, and effort toward learning (Marks, 2000); and the link between teaching and learning (Christensen, 1991, as quoted in Smith, Sheppard, Johnson, & Johnson, 2005); and academic, social, cognitive, and affective factors related to persistence to graduate from high school (Finn & Zimmer, 2013). Some definitions focus on depth as well as categories such as "the behavioral intensity and emotional quality of a student's active involvement during a learning activity" (Jang, Deci, & Reeve, 2010, p. 588).

The definition of the construct is indeed up for debate. Some researchers use engagement and motivation as synonymous (National Research Council and the Institute of Medicine, 2004), while others have argued that engagement describes more than motivation because it must account for active interest, effort, and concentration in schoolwork (Newmann, 1992).

At its core, we believe engagement can be captured by a fairly straight forward definition.

- Engagement is a child's investment in his or her schooling experience (Finn, 1993).

The idea of investment is clear; you put something in with the belief that, after a period of time, you will get an even greater return. The more you believe in this principle, the more you will invest. But to understand what it is about one's schooling experience that makes it worth investing in, more details about engagement need to be clarified.

In just the last few years, general consensus about those details seems to be emerging. In their extensive literature review on the topic titled "School Engagement: Potential of the Concept, State of the Evidence," Fredricks and her colleagues (2004) unified definitions of engagement along three broad constructs: behavioral engagement, emotional engagement, and cognitive engagement.

- Behavioral engagement includes participation in academic and other school activities.
- Emotional engagement includes positive or negative feelings toward teachers, classmates, course work, and school.
- Cognitive engagement includes the learner's investment in learning academic content and developing new skills.

In the most recent and comprehensive scholarly synthesis on the topic, the *Handbook of Research on Student Engagement* (Christenson, Reschly, & Wylie, 2012), these three themes of emotional, behavioral, and cognitive engagement either come up again and again or are stated explicitly.

Table 2.1 presents a summary of the components and measures identified through the Fredricks et al. (2004) review of the engagement literature.

Figure 2.1   Student Engagement

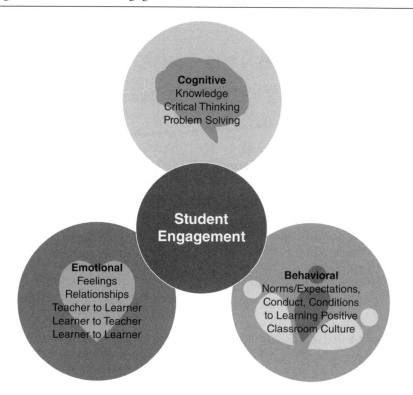

Table 2.1   Student Engagement—Key Aspects of Engagement Identified by Fredricks, Blumenfeld, and Paris (2004)

Behavioral	Emotional	Cognitive
Positive conduct • Follows rules • Adheres to classroom norms Involvement in academic tasks • Effort • Completing tasks • Participation, questions • Extracurricular participation	Affective reactions to work • Enthusiasm or indifference • Feelings about schoolwork Affective reactions to others • Feelings about teachers and peers • Feelings of being valued at school • Identification with school	Investment • Preference for challenge • Effort directed toward learning • Motivation to learn, relevance Strategy • Metacognition • Strategic learning

We will expand on this conceptualization of engagement throughout this chapter.

WHY ENGAGEMENT IS IMPORTANT

Is the primary challenge facing American schools today low achievement or low engagement? Consider the following:

- The United States has a 22 percent dropout rate among high school students (U.S. Department of Education, 2013). Dropping out is associated with unemployment and an increased likelihood for criminal activity.
- Seventy-five percent of high school students say they are bored with their classes (Yazzie-Mintz, 2006). These disengaged students report that they are bored in school because the material is not relevant or because they do not interact with their teachers.
- Engagement decreases each year for students between fifth grade and 12th grade (Gallup, 2014).
- In general, student perceptions of self-competence in school tasks and student perceptions of the value of those tasks decline as they progress from Grade 1 to Grade 12. Specifically, student motivation, perception of ability, and positive attitudes toward school decline through middle school (Epstein & McPartland, 1976; Marsh, 1989) and continue to decline through high school (Jacobs, Lanza, Osgood, Eccles, & Wigfield, 2002).

Edward Deming (2000) states that the first step in transformation is to focus on one's purpose. If the purpose of schools is to improve student learning, how will that occur if students are not interested, let alone invested, in their schooling experience? Improvement initiatives related to student learning are ultimately subject to the perceptions and perspectives of the student themselves. Unfortunately, the perspectives of students are often overlooked by researchers (Gentry, Gable, & Rizza, 2002). In the introduction of their analysis of student perceptions of classroom activities, Gentry and colleagues (2002) contend that:

Evaluation of classroom activities from the students' perspectives is infrequently considered in educational research, school-improvement efforts, and evaluation. (p. 540)

Put simply, if student perceptions matter, they need to be considered in a manner that honors and is responsive to what students are thinking, how they are feeling, and their beliefs about the nature of the work that they are doing. Engagement will precede achievement.

MISTAKING COMPLIANCE FOR ENGAGEMENT

Absent a shared language of engagement, teachers, administrators, and community members often mistake compliance with engagement. Compliance is about adopting a set of behaviors to avoid punishment or get rewards. From a behaviorist perspective, compliance is relatively easy to obtain; reward those who follow the rules, and punish those who don't. But from a humanist perspective, compliance can come at a cost. Individuals may follow the rules but develop animosity toward those who enforce them. Individuals may follow the rules through blind obedience rather than because they think they are important.

Consider two classrooms. In one classroom, all students are seated quietly in their desks. Students are polite. They speak only when asked a question. They ask questions only when they are given permission to do so. They do their work. In the second classroom, students are in motion. They are respectful but are engaged in constant discussion with one another. Occasionally, differences of opinions emerge, and a topic might be debated. Different viewpoints are actively considered over the best process to use to complete a task or project. Students are constantly asking questions of the teacher and of one another. The first classroom is compliant, but these students display close to no passion or enthusiasm for their learning. The second classroom may appear to be chaotic, but these students are actively engaged in learning.

The distinction between behaviors focused on compliance as compared to what we call internal conditions of a learner

Table 2.2   Characteristics of Compliant Classrooms Versus Internal Conditions That Support Engagement

Behaviors as Evidence of Compliance	
Behaviors related to conduct	• Follows rules • Adheres to classroom norms and routines
Behaviors related to completing required academic tasks	• Follows directions • Participates when requested • Asks questions about tasks and requirements • Completes tasks and assignments as requested • Completes assignments on time
Internal Conditions That Support Engagement	
Ownership of learning	• Asks questions about learning • Talks with adults or peers about what he or she is learning in school • Transfers or shares what has been learned to contexts outside of school
Preference for autonomy	• Is self-directed; intentionally chooses to engage in tasks that build skills and understanding • Demonstrates self-control; chooses to avoid behaviors that inhibit skills or prevent understanding • When working with others, acknowledges their need for autonomy
Values and seeks feedback	• Actively seeks feedback to guide efforts to improve • Actively utilizes feedback to modify behavior or understanding • Provides constructive feedback to support others
Commitment to learning	• Perseveres through obstacles by trying new or different strategies • Is tenacious about achieving goals and accomplishing tasks • Supports others' efforts to persevere and achieve
Motivation to learn	• Is assertive about creating opportunities to learn new things or improve existing skills • Takes calculated risks to try new and different strategies to achieve a goal • Encourages others' efforts to persevere and achieve
Pursuit of mastery	• Establishes and pursues challenging, realistic goals • Self-manages action plans for growth in a manner that is conducive to achieving goals • Provides constructive criticism and, if asked, guidance to support others' pursuit of mastery

that support engagement creates a clear distinction between the classrooms that we've accepted as the anachronism of schooling today and the classrooms we'll need to create passionate learners.

Classrooms that are focused on building these internal conditions are the subject of each of the chapters that follow. The purpose and the pathway to moving from compliance to engagement will be described in detail. Before we move there, we need to discuss a few additional ways of thinking about engagement.

A MORE NUANCED VIEW: TYPES OF STUDENT ENGAGEMENT

Typically, engagement is reduced to a dichotomy. Students are either responsible or irresponsible, well behaved or disruptive, present or truant. These either-or propositions seem to imply that engagement is an intrinsic characteristic of the student rather than a set of choices that a student makes depending on how he or she is feeling, his or her level of interest, and his or her belief that, if effort is put forth to accomplish a task, there is a reasonable chance for success. An effective vocabulary for discussing engagement has been adapted from sociologist Robert Merton's work by author Philip Schlechty (2002).

In his seminal work on social structure and perceptions of self, Merton (1949) argued that the relationship between an organization's culture and an individual's actions within that culture could be best understood by understanding the alignment among the organization's goals, the individual's goals, the organization's preferred means to obtain those goals, and the individual's perception of the organization's preferred means. Looking at the interaction among the individual and the organization, Schlechty (2002, 2011) describes five types of engagement.

- Authentic engagement: I accept the organization's goals and the organization's means to attain those goals.
- Passive compliance: I accept the organization's goals, but I reject the means to attain those goals. However, I will comply with the means simply because that is the only way to obtain the organization's goals.

- Ritualistic compliance: I do not accept the goals, but I will comply with the means simply to avoid consequences for failure to follow the rules.
- Retreatism: I accept neither the goals nor the means, and I will not bother anyone in the organization as long as no one bothers me.
- Rebellion: I reject your goals, and I reject your means, and I have created my own set of goals and means while I am at your organization.

Thinking about goals and means provides a robust way of discussing the interrelationship among student behaviors and their resultant engagement.

Too often, educators mistake ritualistic engagement and passive compliance with authentic engagement. This framework helps us

Table 2.3 Building a Shared Language of Engagement: Merton's Typologies as Adapted by Schlechty (2002, 2011)

The Organization's Goals	The Organization's Means	Engagement Typology
Accepts goals	Accepts means	**Authentic Engagement** "My goals and interests match your curriculum."
Accepts goals	Rejects means	**Passive Compliance** "I'll play the game to get good grades or get into college."
Rejects goals	Accepts means	**Ritualistic Compliance** "I'll play the game to avoid negative consequences."
Rejects goals	Rejects means	**Retreatism** "I won't ask anything of you; please don't ask anything of me."
Rejects goals and accepts new goals	Rejects means and accepts new means	**Rebellion** "I can't do your schoolwork and don't want to; I've got other business to tend to here."

think about the reality that some students may walk into class with smiles on their faces and their homework in hand solely because they are playing the game of school. Too often, educators describe students in retreat or rebellion as the source of the problem. Some of the highest-achieving students we've ever seen have placed themselves in retreat or rebellion because of their frustration with the system. They are frustrated that no one understands them. They are frustrated that no one can challenge them. They are frustrated that they are asked to do busywork that they see as irrelevant.

ENGAGEMENT AS MALLEABLE: CLASSROOMS AND SCHOOLS MATTER

As consensus emerges around a definition and the primary components of engagement, consensus is also emerging about some of the key characteristics of the term. Engagement is considered to be contextual and, therefore, malleable. It is influenced by school and classroom culture as well as individual beliefs and needs. This is important because it means that, as educators, we are a key part of the engagement equation.

A critical element of understanding student engagement is the idea that engagement is the result of interaction between a learner and his or her environment. If engagement is contextual, schools can have a direct impact on students' levels and types of engagement. In a study of nearly 3,700 students attending 24 schools, Marks (2000) found that quality reform initiatives that focused on factors such as authentic instruction and supporting student learning substantially influenced student engagement across elementary, middle, and high school samples. Teachers can play a significant role in mitigating the decline of student engagement that typically occurs across the middle school and high school years. In their study on the relationship between engagement and relationships with teachers and peers, Klem and Connell (2004) found that middle school students were "almost three times more likely to report engagement if they experienced highly supportive teachers" (p. 270).

We believe this conceptualization of engagement as a malleable set of emotional, behavioral, and cognitive factors that are related to each student's investment in school provides a practical framework to establish a shared language of student engagement. In our framework for creating passionate learners, the behavioral, emotional, and cognitive components that contribute to and describe engagement should be the starting point to consider each student's reason to invest in his or her schooling experience.

Presently, there are many improvement initiatives underway that can change education and better address the distinct needs of each learner. Educational systems are being redesigned so that learning is visible and personalized to meet students' needs. Community schools are being created where school staff and businesses work together to make connections between the curricular standards and the real world for improved student learning. Continuous improvement systems that use strategies to empower students to give feedback and influence the classrooms are being implemented, and others such as play-based learning, problem-based learning, culturally responsive instruction, and universal design for learning are each examples of educational solutions intended to further engage students. These big attempted solutions that are intended to address current challenges in education can certainly create better-engaged students. In fact, the successful solutions of the future knowingly will incorporate the concepts in our model of creating passionate learners.

The authors believe that, as important as assessment literacy was and continues to be in education, engagement literacy will be of even greater importance into the future. As assessment literacy helped teachers ensure the valid and reliable interpretation and utilization of classroom and large-scale tests, engagement literacy will ensure that students are honored as the key variable in any school reform effort. If we are serious about creating passionate learners, we need to invest more time, effort, and energy to ensure students are supported emotionally, cognitively, and behaviorally in a manner that transcends the system of compliance and test scores that are accepted as successful indicators of schooling today. We believe that the Conceptual Framework for Creating Passionate Learners is the foundation for reform efforts.

To support each child's emotional, behavioral, and cognitive engagement in school as a learner, four key prompts can be used

Figure 2.2   Conceptual Framework for Creating Passionate Learners

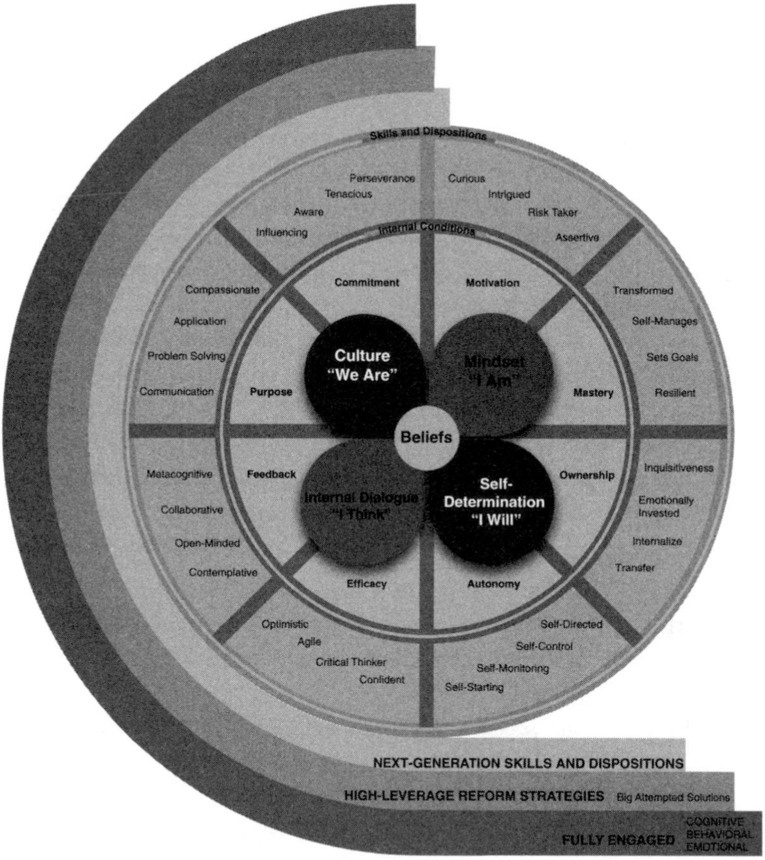

STUDENT
ENGAGEMENT

Emotional engagement includes the students' feelings, interests, and values. When students are emotionally engaged, they will have feelings of belonging and positive attitudes toward school.

Behavioral engagement is how a student conducts himself or herself in the learning process. Behavioral engagement focuses on student participation, work involvement, and conduct.

Cognitive engagement is the investment students put forth to understand complex ideas and wrestle with difficult problems (Fredricks et al., 2004).

to guide our work. *I am, I will, I think,* and *we are* recast the lens of school reform through students' eyes. It is only through students' eyes that our work is valid.

- I am motivated to accomplish tasks. I am able to see the relevancy of learning new content and skills and understand that effort will help me reach my goals (growth mindset).
- I think in productive, positive ways, and I'm responsive to feedback (internal dialogue).
- I will make choices that build my ownership in my learning (self-determination).
- We are committed to finding solutions to problems that are meaningful and filled with purpose (culture).

We believe that a system that utilizes these beliefs will surpass engaging students to creating passionate learners. Passionate learners willingly invest time and effort into learning and do it with a deep desire for learning's sake. Passionate learners connect with something within that is bigger than themselves. The passionate learner has a growth mindset and internal dialogue that reframes his or her thinking toward the positive. Their self-determination helps them make choices that are purposeful. The passionate learner helps build a culture of committed learners who find solutions to problems.

To help create passionate learners, a facilitator or coach is needed, much like the coach at the beginning of this chapter, a coach who based his actions on a humanistic approach. He did not predetermine a runner's ability; instead, he saw each person with capacity to grow in speed and endurance. He did not place focus on winning, trophies, or medals; instead, he talked about the team and the power of running together to help one another achieve success. He did not judge runners on their performance after a practice or meet; instead, he asked questions to diagnose next steps to help his runners meet the personal goals that each created. The coach inherently knew that each runner needed to have cognitive knowledge about form, training, and eating as well as the emotional and social support to succeed. He understood that each runner needed to be truly engaged to do his or her personal best.

CHAPTER 3

The Power of Mindset

*K*ay, a high school girl, ran cross-country, competing in the mile and two-mile events during track season. She exhibited a lot of talent and placed in the top five in major meets. After her junior year, her coach told her he liked watching her run on what he called "pure guts." While she did not have some of her competitors' natural ability, her determination was unmatched. No one had told her that she was not supposed to be among the top runners. She assumed that she should be. She believed that her work and effort would pay off in faster timing. Her thinking determined her attitude, which influenced her behaviors. Psychologist Carol Dweck (2000) calls this relationship among attitude, behaviors, and results *mindset.*

Specifically, this runner exhibited a growth mindset. She sought challenges in practice and competition. When her body did not cooperate during a race, she analyzed her running log from the prior week to see if she needed to change her training strategy. If other runners edged her out, she reflected on what she could learn from them to improve. Her coach was a positive influence, encouraging her to keep a log of miles she ran as related to her strength and endurance. Her coach pointed out subtle corrections, such as hand position or how the swing of an arm can affect the pace of the legs. This student was fortunate to have positive coaching that affected her mindset—and her results.

Another student, Joe, started school with high self-esteem, especially in math. His proud parents told people how smart Joe was. From the time Joe was three, they asked him to perform for guests by solving math problems. They knew Joe was exceptional and often told him how smart he was.

Joe excelled in kindergarten. When he began first grade, his teacher wanted to challenge him appropriately by asking him to use his numeracy skills to solve problems. When Joe couldn't solve a problem instantly, instead of diving in and working through the problem, he used avoidance techniques. He told stories about being smarter than the other students, told his classmates that they were only doing math and he was doing algebra, and when Joe was faced with a problem that looked simple but was unfamiliar to him, he told his teacher he shouldn't solve the problem because it was too easy.

When the teacher asked another student to join Joe for differentiated assignments, Joe became uneasy, especially when the other student was able to solve the problems. Joe was certainly capable of solving the math problems. He was afraid that making a mistake might reveal that he wasn't as smart as others thought; *smart students don't make mistakes.* Joe exhibited a fixed mindset. The teacher provided opportunities to learn new strategies and try new problems, but Joe ignored them. Joe's beliefs about his abilities in math only took him so far. He was unwilling to embrace the struggle and failure that accompanies a growth mindset.

MINDSET

Carol Dweck (2000) and her colleagues have pursued a career's worth of research on whether or not students' beliefs of innate ability or effort contribute to their achievement. The results are the broad discussions on fixed mindset and growth mindset.

A person with a fixed mindset believes he or she is either good at something or not. They perceive their abilities or intelligence as inherent. People who believe they are born with a limited amount of capacity reason that they cannot do a great deal about their own capacity and can only cope with their deficits. This coping mechanism often manifests as avoiding looking dumb (Dweck, 2000).

The story of Joe illustrates the beliefs of a fixed mindset. Joe avoided challenges as they could expose his lack of ability. When he faced an obstacle, he gave up or created reasons why he would not complete the task. Joe did not exert effort in solving tasks as his belief was that effort is a sign of weakness. Joe did not embrace feedback as it played on his fear that, if he did not do something correctly the first time, it might mean he was not smart. In addition, Joe felt threatened when other students succeeded, especially when he struggled (Dweck, 2000). Students with fixed mindsets think, "How can I preserve how others currently see me?" They are not as ready to risk challenges because they initially see potential failure and link that failure to their self-image. If they see themselves as smart or athletic, they want to maintain that image in their own and others' eyes.

A person with a growth mindset believes a person is good at something through practice (Dweck, 2000). People with growth mindsets believe that they are born with enough capacity to excel when effort is exerted. They understand that, the more they do something, the more they improve, and every mistake is an opportunity to learn.

The story of the runner, Kay, demonstrates the beliefs of a growth mindset. Kay perceived challenges as an opportunity to improve. When she faced an obstacle, she assumed she had the skills to overcome it and persisted in her effort. Kay understood that effort equated to a higher level of growth and, in the end, performance. Feedback from her coach and peers was valued, and her peers and competition inspired Kay. Students with growth mindsets think, "My investment in effort now will help me in the future." They see effort as the pathway to growth.

The difference in students' reactions to situations is influenced by whether the student has a fixed mindset or a growth mindset. Licht and Dweck (1984) compared how students with growth as compared to fixed mindsets responded to learning materials they found confusing. The researchers found that students with growth mindsets and students with fixed mindsets thrived at the same rate when they were given clear tasks with little complexity. However, students with growth mindsets outperformed those with fixed mindsets when the tasks they were asked to do were perplexing.

TEACHING TIP

Teachers who emphasize effort over innate ability help nurture a growth mindset. Teachers do this by focusing on a student's personal strengths and giving feedback on the student's effort.

Teachers can share stories and biographies with students about famous people who failed and kept trying to demonstrate how persistence and effort produce success. Walt Disney's studio, Laugh-O-Gram went bankrupt, which left Walt "tougher, more determined, and inured to failure" (Gabler, 2006, p. 73) as he went on to create an enterprise known for thinking out of the box. Elvis Presley waited several months, cut a second demo, and waited months again before Sam Phillips, owner of Memphis Recording Service, decided to record a record with Elvis for Sun Records (Curtin, 1998). Babe Ruth had a record of strikeouts (1,330 strikes) before earning a record 714 home runs (Baseball Almanac, 2000–2014). Teachers and other adults who are important in students' lives can celebrate mistakes and risks students have taken as opportunities for growth in knowledge and power.

If educators support students in adopting growth mindset, then their performance could be enhanced. Blackwell, Trzesniewski, and Dweck (2007) found that students change their self-perception and develop growth mindsets when they learn about the brain. Teachers in the study explained to students that learning meant the students were developing new connections among neurons in their brains. Researchers found that students exposed to this approach increased achievement and were more motivated to learn. "Learners with a growth mindset believe that intelligence is like a muscle—it gets stronger the more it's used" (Downing, 2011, p. 218). The more we exercise our brains, the more neural networks are created and the smarter we become. Not only the smarter we become, but the more capable we see ourselves and the better positioned we are to engage in our learning (Downing, 2011).

In addition, Dweck (2000) and her colleagues found that an adult's focus on student effort has a profound effect on a student's mindset. When adults concentrate on effort and development, students take on growth mindsets and are more apt to take on challenges. Students with growth mindsets believe that hard work and persistence will help them improve. Their inner voices say things like, "I'm not there yet; however, with time and effort, I will grow as a learner or I will develop my ability."

The teachers' efforts to help students understand how to develop their own abilities and change their mindsets resulted in improved student achievement levels and attitudes about their learning processes.

Learners with growth mindsets are more likely to engage in learning. When students are ready to take on new challenges and feel free to fail, they let go of others' expectations and are free to question, ponder, and reflect—to truly learn. Growth mindsets give learners permission to wrestle with a problem that cannot be solved instantaneously.

A belief in a growth mindset will change how students perceive themselves and their own world. "I am" represents how each student who has a growth mindset would say to him- or herself, "I am capable of improving my skills and abilities in any area where I choose to focus." The conditions under a growth mindset that support passionate learning include both motivation and mastery.

Figure 3.1   Growth Mindset—"I Am"

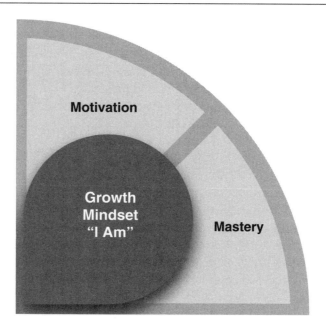

Figure 3.2   Motivation and Mastery Defined

Term	Definition
Motivation	"Inherent tendency to seek out novelty and challenges, to extend and exercise their capabilities, to explore, and to learn" (Ryan & Deci, 2000)
Mastery	Allows learners to become better at something that matters to them, to learn and create new things beyond expected learning targets (Pink, 2009)

When students have growth mindsets, their motivation extends their learning. They embrace challenge and accept setbacks as normal in growth. The motivation and effort put forth lead students on a course to mastery. When students are on this path, they enter a state of flow, where they become so involved in the learning process, "that nothing else seems to matter" (Csikszentmihalyi, 1990, p. 4).

Motivation is a product of mindset. Daniel Pink (2009), author of *Drive: The Surprising Truth About What Motivates Us*, names three elements that lead to high, engaging motivation. The motivation elements include autonomy, mastery, and purpose. Autonomy allows individuals to give input into the task; mastery is an individual's desire to get better at something; and purpose is the desire for an individual to serve in a way that is beyond self (Pink, 2009). If the three elements combined are what motivate an individual, then as educators, the following questions should be asked: How do we develop autonomy? How can we build pathways to mastery? How can we help students see purpose? And how are autonomy, mastery, and purpose interdependent in student success?

TEACHING TIP

Ideas for motivating students may include the following:

- **Consider opportunities for social interaction.** Introduce structured, focused, cross-age peer tutoring, cooperative learning groups, and informal study groups.
- **Providing audiences for student work.** Expect students to submit their work to publications, post it on Web sites, present it to live audiences, or present it to guest experts.

- **Reduce the effort needed to complete an academic assignment.** The amount of effort needed to undertake an activity (effort threshold) will play an important role in motivation. Break tasks down into smaller, easier-to-accomplish steps that are combined as a final product.
- **Connect academic requirements to real-world situations.** The media are full of true stories that demonstrate the application of knowledge from various academic areas to real-world problems. Taught content, assignments, and homework can be put through a relevant lens.
- **Make learning engaging.** Mix things up, get them out of their seats, or play academic vocabulary games. Humor and fast-paced instruction are also methods for making learning more lively and interesting. At times, we forget how developmentally young they really are . . .

Students are naturally motivated in things that matter to them. When individuals find joy in the journey and pursuit of becoming better at something that matters to them, then they are in a state of working toward mastery. A growth mindset is necessary for an individual to understand that effort is necessary to reach mastery. To move to an expert level of performance requires deliberate practice, repeated practice focused on specific aspects of performance, and feedback on that performance and modification (Ericsson, 2006). Passion coupled with ability can lead to a drive toward mastery.

POWER OF EFFORT

Differences in cultures around the world have manifested into firm beliefs regarding effort and ability. Harold Stevenson and Rick Stigler (1992) first researched the effects of focusing on ability versus focusing on effort in a study of American, Chinese, and Japanese cultures. They found that American culture emphasizes innate abilities, while the Chinese and Japanese cultures emphasize effort. The differences are manifested in each culture's language and self-talk. At an American wedding reception, one man said he would not dance because he "just was not good at it." That's the same claim many students and adults use about their abilities in math, writing, or art. Their research found that Americans were more likely to speak as though people are born with certain abilities and cannot change their capacities in these areas. Conversely, Stevenson and Sigler found that people from Japan or China are more likely to disagree with the idea that a person is not good at a task because of innate ability. Cultures that emphasize effort view the absence of a skill as simply a lack of opportunity to learn or the need for additional time to practice.

Malcolm Gladwell (2008) cites Singapore, South Korea, Taiwan, Hong Kong, and Japan as cultures that emphasize work ethic. Students in these countries demonstrate greater persistence than American students due to a different set of assumptions about the link among capacity, effort, and results.

Further supporting these differences, Blinco's (1993) findings suggest that Japanese students are persistent due to early focus on effort in their homes coupled with a focus on effort in schools, resulting in reaching goals through tenacity. The outcome is better scores on the Trends for International Mathematics and Science Study (TIMMS) assessment, which measures not only knowledge but also students' tenacity in resolving difficult problems. Americans have more of a fixed mindset about intelligence than other cultures throughout the world.

What does research show about effort? Robert Marzano, Debra Pickering, and Jane Pollock (2001) found that effort has a 0.80 effect size on student learning.

TEACHING TIP

The strong effect size of effort should encourage adults to shift emphasis to help students reflect on their effort and internalize the resulting outcomes. Dean, Hubbell, Pitler, and Stone (2012) suggest a simple instructional change: Ask students to write down what they learn as a result of a lesson or experience, perhaps also including what they will do to practice the new skill. Another strategy in shifting the focus to effort is for the teacher to comment on a student's effort and give specific feedback focused on the strategy the student used to solve a problem. The net results of focusing and commenting on effort can greatly enhance the way a student approaches learning.

LEVERAGING MINDSET

Essential to the educator's lens is to join students in looking to their future in being college, career, and life ready. Every aspect of creating passionate learners is incredibly important to school-age children and equally important to life far beyond school. The knowledge, skills, and dispositions related to creating passionate learners must be viewed as transferable from school to life. A fixed mindset does not mean that a person cannot be successful, but it can mean that someone may not mature into his or her full potential. Take Alex, who is in upper management. He is smart, speaks articulately, and is creative in the workplace. He has a lot of great things happening under his leadership; however, Alex has a difficult time when given any type of feedback for self-improvement—professionally and personally. When he has been approached about thinking about doing things differently, he instantly finds an excuse to why he has done things his way. If someone has an idea and implements it successfully, Alex is quick to find fault with the idea or the person. If Alex changed his mindset, he could grow to a great leader.

Maggie is also in a leadership role. When you ask her what brought her to this point, she shares the names of people who influenced her and talks about long hours of reading and applying what she learned. She is not afraid to say that she has learned many important lessons along the way and realizes that life is a continuous learning process where one grows from mistakes. When new, difficult tasks are brought to her, she takes the tasks on with a sense of determination. Maggie asks her team to reflect on projects, in services, and so on, so that improvement can be made in the future. In all, Maggie and her team work as a unit, using each other's strengths, to make the organization better.

Both of these people are finding success in the workplace; however, they have different outlooks on their own lives and the people who surround them as a result of their mindsets. What is the effect of each of these mindsets on the individual? What is the effect of the mindset of the leader on the coworkers in the organization? What is the effect of mindset on the followers in the organization? When one reflects on the ripple effect of a person's mindset on the individual as well as the individuals around them, it is astounding. Mindset can make or break a life. The way individuals perceive the world can make a difference in their lives.

A growth mindset is a necessary attribute to successfully navigate the various roles in life. Downing (2011) states that "if you've developed a growth mindset, you have a core belief that will help you achieve success in college and beyond" (p. 219). A growth mindset is a priority life skill and an attribute that needs to be understood by educators and students.

CHANGING OUR MENTAL MODELS ABOUT MINDSET TO AFFECT STUDENT ENGAGEMENT

Maria is a teacher who learned about growth and fixed mindsets in a workshop. In the beginning, she reflected on herself and realized that, in some areas, she had a growth mindset and, in others, a fixed mindset. When she thought about her fixed mindset regarding math, she quickly summed up her life and how she avoided math at any cost. The thought struck her how she could perhaps make a difference for the students she taught.

Maria taught her students about fixed and growth mindset and the effect each has on thoughts and choices. She was cognizant to remind students that, if they were struggling, it was great news because of the neural connections their brains were making. She modeled in her own life the way she was changing her mindset in math and the positive messages she told herself when she was faced with figuring out problems. Examples of real people who failed and kept on trying were shared as well as the 10,000-hour rule (Gladwell, 2008), which links expert performance not to innate abilities but to years of focused, deliberate practice in a specific domain (Ericsson et al., 1993). In all, she wanted her students to understand that effort equaled improved outputs. The students in Maria's classroom self-reflected on their own effort put forth anchored against their results. They took pride in how their efforts moved their personal needle to improve learning.

TEACHING TIP

Students keep track of their effort put forth in relation to their learning. Students can use an Effort Tracker as a tool to monitor effort. The tool helps students reflect on their effort and learning, specifically how their effort improves their skill and understanding. See Appendix.

EFFICIENCY FOR ADULTS AND EFFECTIVENESS FOR STUDENTS

Many successful teachers feel held back by the limiting structures they operate within, such as the calendar, student credit requirements, length of class periods, days, school year, and so on. These limiting conditions have fostered an educational climate resulting in instructional approaches being efficient for adults but not necessarily effective for students.

Students may appreciate a teacher's knowledge, but if teachers have little regard for students' learning styles, students may have a difficult time learning or understanding the material. One student said she had loved social studies until she had a teacher who lectured every day for 50 minutes and she discovered the notes she took on his lectures did not match the assessments.

Successful teachers realize that they must make an impact on every student they work with. They understand that relationships are key, that they must use strategies to make learning relevant, and that they must engage students in lessons that students want to be a part of. As Jim Rickabaugh (2011) stated, "Every level we don't get it right with a student has a compounding impact on each level after."

Educators make sure they get it right by planning lessons based on what will keep students engaged and part of the learning process. Teaching is not something they do to students but how they welcome students, involve them in the process, and use what is known about the brain to keep students actively engaged, so they come to school excited to participate actively in learning.

MAKING LEARNER PSYCHOLOGY RELEVANT

Educators have had courses in preservice and graduate school in educational psychology, child psychology, adolescent psychology, and possibly organizational or industrial psychology. That knowledge can be used to shift focus to student engagement. Every preservice teacher learns about Lev Vygotsky, who believed learning is an active and collaborative process drawn from the individual's interpretation of knowledge constructed from experience. Interpreting Vygotsky's statement through the student engagement lens, educators can understand the importance of accessing student's prior knowledge and experiences. Prior knowledge and experiences allow students to make more meaningful connections between teacher and learner, between prior content and process, and between future content and process.

Vygotsky (1978) said a student can use oral language to talk through a task to help that child complete a task. This is referred to as *self-talk* and helps the children facilitate their own behaviors. Teachers who know the importance of student self-talk in completing a task encourage students to talk throughout the day to get the can-do messages they can facilitate through their own speech. Powerful, positive self-talk helps shape mindset. Teachers model activities that are at the cutting edge of a student's ability, so students are able to apply the strategy or skill by themselves. Vygotsky (1978) says students can imitate only what is within their developmental level. He calls this the *zone of proximal development.* Effective teachers use formative and summative assessments to understand what the students know to teach the students the next steps of what they need to know.

Leading students to a mindset in which they understand the role and importance of effort requires care and intentionality. Teachers shape students' thinking and, like the runner in the story at the beginning of this chapter, their thinking can change their behaviors and attitudes. When students develop growth mindsets, they take risks and persist when faced with challenges. When teachers create a climate of trust and appreciate the gifts each student brings to the classroom, they set a tone of inclusiveness that encourages students' risk taking. Psychology supports understanding how students learn so that teachers can advance student progress. Creating an environment to develop mindset begins with using the skills and tools we are given.

MIGRATING FROM A FIXED TO A GROWTH MINDSET

Knowing about fixed and growth mindsets is important; causing movement toward a growth mindset is even more important. Each of us has such power to help a student migrate to either a growth mindset or a fixed mindset. We can help or hurt by our beliefs, words, and actions. The messages we share as well as what we emphasize in our teaching and conversations can have a dramatic influence on student mindsets. When we think of the power an individual teacher has with a student, think bulldozer, think tidal wave, think inspiration. Yes, teacher power could be likened to the equivalent of all those things.

Jackie was a student who was on the verge of dropping out of junior high school. She struggled in all of her subject areas, but she struggled especially hard in the area of math. When things became difficult, she grew to think it was easier to say wisecracks to the teacher and create disruptions in class as a way to cover up her struggles. Entering her freshman year, she began using the same antics as she had in the past to avoid people discovering her inadequacies in math. At this time, her teacher worked from the first day to try to get to know Jackie. The teacher wanted to know what lay just beneath the surface with this child. Why did Jackie behave the way she did? What was really the root cause of her daily distractions? The math teacher went out of her way to find Jackie in study hall to make a connection and ask how things were going. It took a while; however, at some point fairly early on, Jackie felt this was a person she could trust. It was this trust that allowed the teacher to begin to reach this child in ways others had not been able to.

The teacher did individual math assessments to find out exactly what gaps Jackie had. The teacher found the gaps and began to tutor Jackie to make up that gap. The tutoring showed some indications that slight progress was taking place; however, the math teacher soon realized that a deeper, more critical issue needed their joint attention. The teacher had a strong hunch that Jackie stopped believing in herself as a learner, and those beliefs had to be addressed in order to make the necessary catch-up. Jackie had to see how the issue was not her ability but that she had not given herself the opportunity to learn some of the key strategies that she needed. The teacher shared that, if Jackie put in the time and effort, she would see growth in her understanding of math. The teacher and Jackie discussed how attitude toward learning, effort, and focus would influence how she did in math. The teacher encouraged her to stay focused on attitude and effort and said, "Let's just see what happens."

The teacher obviously had high expectations, but she knew that, if she could cause movement in Jackie on the mindset continuum, her math results would soon follow. The teacher used a math assessment to establish a baseline and began to graph Jackie's achievement. Each week, the teacher gave a short assessment on the concepts that Jackie was working on, and she would show her the growth. Each day, the teacher helped Jackie self-reflect on the effort that Jackie put in during the tutoring session as well as any extra time at home devoted to learning. It was through this process that Jackie began to see that time and effort put into math had a direct link to how she was improving. It was through this process that Jackie began to view herself through a new lens. Jackie saw herself as capable both as a learner and successful in math. In essence, she had migrated her mindset from fixed to growth. This situation that Jackie found herself in is not unique. The fact that this teacher had an understanding of mindsets was the tidal wave of support this student needed in order to be inspired to see what she was truly capable of. Downing (2011) states, "If you realize you've developed a fixed mindset, you aren't stuck with it. You can revise your mindset" (p. 219).

We can all relate to stories we have witnessed, been part of, or personally experienced where a switch in mindset was the variable that caused a dynamic change in outcome. We all feel great about those stories and are proud of the person who made the switch and happy for his or her success. What do we need to understand about the environment, the strategies, and the human connection so that these successes are capable and can be replicated in other students?

In reality, students' mindsets naturally can be placed at various points on a continuum, from fixed mindset to growth mindset. Each student will enter this continuum at a different point and most likely be at different point in the continuum for different realms during life. For example, Kevin has a growth mindset in athletics such as basketball but a fixed mindset in math. His teacher can use this as an opportunity to help Kevin figure out what attributes in his growth mindset in basketball can be transferred to math to help him be successful. Questions such as these will help: How often do you play basketball during recess, after school, or on weekends? How often do you pay attention to others who play basketball to learn new techniques and skills? If you put in additional time in math, what do you think may happen to your ability in math? If you pay attention to how classmates solve problems and try out those techniques, how might that help you understand math?

Fixed Mindset   Growth Mindset

$$\longleftrightarrow$$

Now that we know what we know about the power of mindset, accepting where students naturally fall on the continuum is unacceptable practice for us as adults. Therefore, we have an obligation to help students assess where they are and create the conditions where they can begin their personal migration toward an enhanced growth mindset.

STUDENT EXERCISE TO ENHANCE GROWTH MINDSET—GRADES 5–12

Have students in your class interview an adult in their life. Give them the following guidelines:

- Share with the adult that you are learning about how to persevere through the tough issues that life can throw at each of us.
- More specifically share that you are learning how your attitude, beliefs, and effort can make the difference in working through these challenges.
- Ask the adult the following questions:
  - Describe something you faced in life that was a big challenge.
  - Why was it important for you to succeed with this issue?

(Continued)

(Continued)

- Ask the adult to share some of the details surrounding the context of that challenge so that you feel as though you are right there in the middle of that challenge. More specifically ask about the people present, variables they had to contend with, opinions of the people, risks taken, and how they felt in the middle of the challenge?
- Ask what was at stake.
- Ask what strategies they used to help solve the issue.
- Ask how important their attitude and effort were.
- Ask if they would do anything different today.
  - Ask how they felt about how the issue turned out.

Following the individual activity conducted by each student, have students share their interview stories with the class. In each case, paraphrase to students what you heard them say, and ask the students probing questions. Have the class empathize with the person's situation. Ask the students what they would have done in a similar situation. Also, ask the students what they would do differently now that they have studied growth mindsets. The following activity will extend the learning and provide students with an opportunity to go deeper in their understanding. An activity that would follow nicely is having the students reflect on a time when they wished a situation could have turned out better. This reflection will further draw out from the students a deep understanding of the need to migrate their mindsets (see box).

KEY QUESTIONS TO GUIDE STUDENT SELF-REFLECTION

- Did I personally work hard enough?
- Can I work harder?
- Can I change my current strategy slightly?
- Do I need completely new strategies?

- Do I need to clarify the feedback that I am giving to my teacher on what I understand and what instruction I need next?
- Can I change my attitude?
- If I cannot change my attitude, can I change my approach?
- Can networking and collaborating with my fellow classmates help with my current learner block?
- What is one thing I could do personally to make this learning experience more enjoyable and relevant?
- If I practiced changes toward a growth mindset could it become a habit for me?
- If I charted my attitude, effort, and improvements in learning, would the findings be accurate, and could I change the trend?

By having the students ask and answer these self-reflection questions, we help create the conditions where we join forces with the students in causing a mindset migration.

THE IMPLICATIONS OF GROWTH MINDSET FOR EMOTIONAL, BEHAVIORAL, AND COGNITIVE ENGAGEMENT

Growth mindset directly relates to emotional, behavioral, and cognitive engagement in students' learning. When educators and staff in a building understand the power of a growth mindset, the words that they choose to greet and teach students will be done in a way that influences their emotional engagement. Words that focus on effort and emphasize that feedback are necessary for learner growth. It's not simply about getting an A but about learning for learning's sake and understanding and applying learning to life's situations. Emotional engagement is enhanced when educators value students' thinking and build a community of support.

The characteristics of a growth mindset include embracing challenge, persistence in the face of setbacks, effort to gain mastery, and feedback to grow as a learner (Dweck, 2006). Behavioral engagement is attended to when teachers help students understand the characteristics of a growth mindset and give opportunities for students to embrace challenging work.

The growth mindset characteristics also have a direct impact on cognitive engagement. When teachers give time for students to self-reflect and monitor the amount of effort given, encourage flexibility in solving problems, and create a culture where taking risks in learning is evident, it provides a venue for students to understand the importance of learning for learning sake.

THE IMPORTANCE OF DISPOSITIONS

"Dorothy was admired for her modesty, dignity, and class. She was respected for her concern for others, was loved by her family and friends, and returned that love with a warm heart." These are the words that were written about a woman who had recently passed away. The words described her character, and her character was her legacy.

Andrea Bocelli, an Italian singer known for his beautiful tenor voice, found that music had a calming effect on his life from an early age. Andrea describes how he loved a challenging piece of music and enjoyed performing. With some pressure from his family, he pursued a law degree, but his passion was still performing music. It was his tenacity and "refusal to accept defeat" that allowed him worldwide success as a performer today (Felix, 2001, p. 45). In Bocelli, Foster, Schwartz, Foster, and Skylark's (2006) song "Because We Believe," the lyrics affirm this tenacity: "Look ahead and never turn your back on the caress of your dreams." Persistence and tenacity were keys to Bocelli's success.

Vince Lombardi, the Green Bay Packer head coach from 1958 to 1967, who led his team to six division titles, five National Football League (NFL) championships, and two Super Bowls (I and II) wins is a legend to fans in Wisconsin. He taught and enforced key principles with his players including commitment, teamwork, discipline, willpower, leadership, mental toughness, passion, confidence, truth, faith, and habit. These key principles were how he led his life and what he is remembered for.

Coach Lombardi shared the following wise words to his team: "Watch your thoughts; they become your beliefs. Watch your beliefs; they become your words. Watch your words; they become your actions. Watch your actions; they become your habits. Watch your habits; they become your character"

(Family of Vince Lombardi, 2010). In schools, we want to influence the character of our students. We can do this by taking a page from Vince Lombardi to teach key principles. The authors feel that key principles described by Vince Lombardi or a broader set of skills and dispositions are needed to help students become successful. Dispositions are the tendencies toward a particular pattern that becomes a habit of mind (Costa & Kallick, 2014; Dickmann & Stanford-Blair, 2009; Katz, 1993) and skills are the disposition in action.

DISPOSITIONS: NOW AND IN THE FUTURE

Many state academic standards currently focus on critical thinking, problem solving, and analytical skills. These are skills that will inspire students so that they are ready for the vigor of college and realistic, demanding careers. One area that has not been addressed completely is teaching students the skills and dispositions they need in order to critically think, collaborate, communicate, and creatively problem solve.

Change is a constant in today's world, and students need to be equipped to adjust to change by learning how to develop dispositions that will help them make the most of their potential to succeed. Art Costa and Bena Kallick (2014), authors of *Learning and Leading With Habits of Mind* and *Dispositions: Reframing Teaching and Learning,* share how the "focus is not only learning *of* the content but also learning *from* the content (p. 3), thus intentionally being mindful of modeling and teaching dispositions. Costa and Kallick go on to argue that dispositions need to be at the core of curricular design.

A word of caution is not to teach a disposition of the week, as that is a transactional change that will not truly develop dispositions in the students; however, it will give them the vocabulary of what it is.

> Dispositions to learning should be key performance indicators of the outcomes of schooling. Many advocates for large scale assessments believe that, if achievement is enhanced, there is a ripple effect to these dispositions. However such a belief is not defensible. Such dispositions need planned interventions. (Hattie, 2009, p. 40)

When one makes a transformational change, it is a rethinking of how we do something. Therefore, it truly is a rethinking of how we frame classrooms so that dispositions are expected and can be demonstrated and practiced by students.

DISPOSITIONS NESTED IN THE FRAMEWORK FOR CREATING PASSIONATE LEARNERS

Educators have information at their fingertips but may be overwhelmed by the increasing amounts of information being shared. Costa and Kallick (2014) state, "We are living in an era of increasing uncertainty, complexity, and ambiguity in which we are bombarded with conflicting models of what to value, what to believe, how to decide, and how to live" (p. 8). The Framework for Creating Passionate Learners begins with the four beliefs of mindset, internal dialogue, self-determination, and culture. We argue that these four beliefs will make a direct impact on teachers' and students' core inputs as well as the outcomes of education.

There is a synergy among these four factors. A growth mindset opens up a host of possibilities to see oneself as a learner. A growth mindset is supported by internal dialogue the students use to determine whether or not they will approach tasks. The teacher can help develop this by using words in an intentional and purposeful way. The feedback and reflective questions open the door to students' efficacy about their behaviors, outlooks, and mental attitudes. Self-determination empowers students to create their goals and self-direct their learning. The autonomy and ownership a student brings to a classroom experience result in intrinsic motivation that will not only lead a student to be more engaged in the classroom but also committed to lifelong learning. Finally, culture sets the tone where students are empowered to use these components as priorities.

At the periphery of the Framework for Creating the Passionate Learners is a set of skills and dispositions that can be taught, reflected upon, monitored, and celebrated. Learners are more likely to be passionate about learning both in school and in life. We believe from our experiences with classroom teachers that, as dispositions are understood and strengthened, those efforts underpin and result in increased achievement. The remaining portion of this chapter is devoted to dispositions that align with each of the beliefs of the framework. Additionally, the skills and dispositions are defined, and strategies to strengthen those dispositions are suggested.

GROWTH MINDSET DISPOSITIONS

Gloria was a student who experienced success early on. She found that math and science came easily to her, excelled at gymnastics, and loved playing the violin. School was going well for her until she got to high school. To her parent's dismay, they found that she was not doing well. Home life became more difficult as her parents had to press her to do her homework and study, and it left them wondering what went wrong.

Exasperated, they went to one of Gloria's teachers from the prior year to see if she had any insight to help them in their struggle. The teacher listened to what was happening and began to reflect on what she knew about growth mindset. She noted that the parents talked about how Gloria gave up easily and made excuses when she encountered challenging assignments. The teacher asked questions and shared information on growth and fixed mindsets. As the parents heard about a fixed mindset, they exclaimed that the fixed mindset phrases were describing their daughter.

The teacher gave Gloria the student version of Carol Dweck's mindset quiz. This step helped the teacher give purpose to learning about fixed and growth mindsets and how the brain works. Through the week, Gloria and her classmates learned about self-talk and how to develop a growth mindset. In the weeks that followed, the discussion opened up the opportunity to learn about additional dispositions that fit into the category of mindset. These are shown in Figure 3.3.

Students who have growth mindsets will perceive their environment and world differently. They understand that effort makes a difference in their performance; that it is normal to be challenged by an idea, concept, or task; and that with effort and persistence, they can overcome the challenge. A growth mindset opens up the possibility of dispositions that will help students in their learning.

Figure 3.3 Growth Mindset Through the Teacher's Eyes

Skills and dispositions to support key components of motivation **"I can reach the goals I set for myself"**	Students with growth mindsets believe they can grow their abilities. They take risks, are curious, approach the unknown with a sense of intrigue, and are assertive about solving problems.		
	Skills/ Dispositions	**Defined as**	**Supported by teachers who . . .**
	Curious "I can want to learn more"	A strong yearning to know, learn, and understand something (Engel, 2013)	. . . give students choice, which helps them connect with material and subject areas that they are naturally curious about. Susan Engel (2013) shares the following key ideas to increase curiosity: • Count the number of questions students ask (this brings an awareness to the number and quality of student questions). • Give time for students to find answers. • Teachers keep track of the number of opportunities that students are given to figure out what they need or want to know.
	Intrigued "I can explore and learn new things"	A strong interest in something	. . . speak to the importance of teaching by doing so that students observe their teacher engaged in wrestling with a process, issue, or problem (Kohn, 2004). When teachers are able to model their intrigue, students will have a better understanding of the process of intrigue.

Risk taker "I can try new things with confidence"	Taking on a task that is on the "edge of one's competence" (Costa & Kallick, 2014, p. 23)	. . . create an environment where students feel supported and encouraged even if they fail in a task. . . . create an environment where students are encouraged to "fail forward." Johnson-Smith (2005) shares the following advice: • Tell students the climate of risk taking desired in the classroom—applaud imperfect attempts. • Demonstrate risk taking, and explain people get better by taking calculated risks. • Demonstrate trying something that you are terrible at. • Create a culture where classmates applaud risk taking.
Assertive "I can share my viewpoint respectfully"	Respectfully and confidentially communicating one's views and ideas (Kolb & Stevens-Griffith, 2009)	. . . encourage the articulation of ideas and opinions. Students are taught how to share a viewpoint respectfully. Kolb and Stevens-Griffith (2009) suggest to teach techniques for saying no when the students are requested to do something inappropriate or unsafe as well as practice assertive communications including the following: • Using a calm voice • Using I statements • Sharing feelings as a result of the behavior • Discussing the preferred outcome (Kolb & Stevens-Griffith, p. 33) in advance

(Continued)

Figure 3.3 (Continued)

Skills and dispositions to support key components of mastery "I can become excellent at this"	Skills/ Dispositions	Defined as	Supported by teachers who . . .
	Transformed "I can achieve because I believe"	The ability to use new beliefs about capacity and new skills and understanding to be more effective than what was once thought possible	. . . provide choice, allow opportunities for goal setting, and ensure time, dialogue, and self-reflection. Intentionally foster a sense of belonging or relatedness (Furrer & Skinner, 2003).
	Self-Manages "I can do it myself"	The conscious choice to take responsibility for one's behaviors without assistance from others (Lan, 2005)	. . . assess their students' ability to self-manage, they share expectations, model behaviors, give feedback to the student as well as time for the student to reflect. Young children benefit from a visual reminder of the expectations. Zumbrunn, Tadlock, and Roberts (2011) found in their review of the literature the following strategies for self-monitoring learning: • Students set goals and create plans to reach them. • Students keep track of learning toward goal. • Help students create an awareness of attention control. • Students use learning strategies to understand material. • Students self-evaluate their learning.

54

Sets Goals "I can set and reach my goals"	Creating a vision of where one wants to be and concentrating one's efforts in order to reach the vision through goal setting	. . . set aside time for students to reflect on their work, set goals, and monitor their progress on the goals they set. Schunk and Rice's (1991) study found the following: • Specific feedback from the teacher to the goal increased a student's self-efficacy and achievement. • Process goals (applying knowledge) increased students understanding and efficacy. Schunk (2009) recommends teachers help students: • Focus on process goals • Create goals that are specific and on a student's proximal development • Divide long-term goals into smaller short-term goals
Resilient "I can adapt to what life brings me"	The ability to overcome and adapt to challenging life experiences and give a "positive response to failure or adversity" (Perkins-Gough, 2013, p. 14)	. . . have students, if they make mistakes, problem solve how they will help themselves in the future. . . . admit if they make a mistake or overreact to a situation and demonstrate their own strategies to change their own behaviors in the future. Sagor (1996) states that, to build resilient students and build for their future success, focus on the following student capacities: • Competence • Belonging • Usefulness • Potency • Optimism Henderson (2013) states that adults need to help students know and understand their strengths as well as create a caring and supportive environment.

In each of these dispositions, the teacher needs to foster the strengths in students. Under the category of motivation are dispositions such as curiosity, intrigue, risk taker, and assertiveness. In order to grow and enhance these dispositions, the teacher must be able to see the positives of when a student is passionate about a project and wants to continue working even though it is time to move into another subject, or that, when a student tries out an experiment in science that didn't turn out well, it was curiosity that caused him or her to take a risk, or when a student respectfully voices an opinion in social studies that does not match the opinion of the teacher. In each of these cases, the students are using dispositions that can inspire them in the classroom as well as be a strength in life. As the adult, we need to recognize this opportunity and help the students in the classroom while they are displaying the disposition.

In the area under mastery, the dispositions of transformed, self-management, goal setting, and resilience start with helping the student see each day as a new beginning of possibilities, regardless of events that happened the prior day. The teacher can send the message that today is a new day; self-talk in a positive way can change mindset.

CLASSROOM STRATEGIES FOR STRENGTHENING STUDENT DISPOSITIONS

When students are focused on dispositions, they are mindful of the dispositions they are exhibiting and can make active choices to adopt certain behaviors. If a teacher, school, or district is effective with teaching and growing dispositions, this is a way to work smarter, not harder, in our effectiveness as educators.

As with any systemic change, staff has to be given opportunities to learn, support, grow, and be committed to the work. The work begins with staff understanding the Framework for Creating Passionate Learners and becoming comfortable with a common vocabulary that will be utilized by staff and students. From there, staff members meet collaboratively to discuss implementing the beliefs and dispositions as central to their lesson designs and thoughtfully reflect on what dispositions they possess as teachers and how to deliberately model them and set up their classroom to grow them. Costa and Kallick (2014) state that "few people, however, are aware that the maps they use to take action are not the theories they explicitly espouse" (p. 12). For example, teachers can say they want students to be persistent when solving a math problem or be self-directive in their learning; however, if they do not give the time necessary for students to struggle and persist with a problem or they set up the guidelines on what the students will do within a set time, it is difficult for students to experience the practice needed to become persistent or self-directed learners.

Some questions for teachers and staff members to self-reflect on in order to create an environment conducive to building dispositions while moving their own personal needles forward include the following:

- Why do I care about dispositions for myself and for my students?
- What dispositions are strengths for me to model?
- What dispositions do I naturally exhibit on a daily basis?
- How will I manage modeling dispositions needed for my individual students?
- How will I value dispositions in my classroom? In our school? In our district?

Once staff members are knowledgeable about their own dispositions, they can become more cognizant about the status of their students' dispositions. The first step is to bring awareness to students about dispositions and the related habits of thinking that positively influence actions. Second, teachers and staff will want to integrate lessons regarding the teaching of dispositions into normal, everyday instruction. Some teachers will use the curriculum or content area to highlight and connect a disposition of a person that is being studied, while others will choose to discuss how a disposition might be practiced in the next project, activity, or process. Next, the teacher gives mindful feedback to the student so that it causes metacognition in students regarding their own growth in dispositions. Finally, giving time for students to self-assess their dispositions, both those that are strengths and those they would like to develop further, is necessary. Through teaching, modeling, conferring, and giving feedback to students, a shift in dispositions occurs.

Students can monitor their own growth and dispositions by discussing, writing, or conferring about their dispositions using the student self-reflection tool in Figure 3.5.

Figure 3.4   Growth Mindset—"I Am"

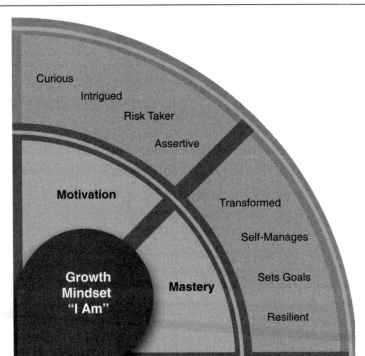

HOW GROWTH MINDSET SUPPORTS PASSIONATE LEARNERS

This chapter began with a story of a runner who, through the help of her coach, developed a growth mindset. Examples also were provided by learners who had developed fixed mindsets and the difficulties those fixed mindsets caused related to their outlooks and learning. In short, a growth mindset matters. Teacher knowledge of mindset and his or her intentional action with students matter even more. Growth mindset is the first step in helping students become passionate learners.

Our education systems can be efficient for adults, or they can be more student centered and effective for learners. If a person is deemed to have a fixed mindset, he or she can, with support, migrate to a growth mindset. A student's reflection all along that migration is central to influencing internal dialogue, which is discussed in Chapter Four.

Figure 3.5 Internal Conditions of Motivation and Mastery That Result in Passionate Learning

	MINDSET			
	Indifferent	Compliant	Engaged	Passionate
Curious	I am able to choose to do an activity that does not involve learning something new if given an opportunity to explore an idea or concept.	I am able to come to class and participate in what I am asked to do.	I am able to learn and understand something because I have such a strong yearning to know more.	I am motivated to learn new things. I approach learning with a mindset to be assertive, intrigued, curious, and a risk taker.
Intrigue	I am able to come to school but I am not interested in exploring new topics or ideas.	I am able to focus my efforts on the work the teacher assigns to me.	I am able to explore opportunities that I have a strong interest in.	
Risk Taker	I am able to come to school and follow the routines and procedures that are set up. I do not feel safe to take a risk.	I am able to try out a new strategy or skill when I am directed to do so.	I am comfortable trying out new ideas, strategies, or skills.	
Assertive	If I am confronted with a challenge, I assume it can't be solved and do not ask for help.	I am able to ask questions about dates, deadlines, and so on.	I am assertive about finding answers when I have questions I am curious about.	

(Continued)

Figure 3.5 (Continued)

		MINDSET		
	Indifferent	Compliant	Engaged	Passionate
Transformed	I am fine with how things are presently.	I am able to do what is expected in class.	I am able to see myself in a positive way. I have changed my behaviors and choices to become healthier in mind and body.	I am a person who understands that motivation and effort put forth lead me to mastery. I approach learning with the goal to transform my learning, self-manage, set goals, and be resilient.
Self-Manages	I am comfortable being a follower.	I am able to manage myself so that I do not get in trouble.	I am able to self-manage my behaviors and take responsibility for my actions without assistance from others.	
Sets Goals	I am fine with living day to day without a set of goals.	I am able to set a goal when I am asked to do so by the teacher, but I do not use goal setting to accomplish my own personal goals.	I am able to set goals and reflect on my progress.	
Resilient	I am fearful of the personal anxiety from stress.	I am able to do what an adult asks me to do to improve at the task if I fail at something.	I am able to think positively when faced with adversity or failure.	

CHAPTER 4

Internal Dialogue

*Reengage Learners
Using Teacher Feedback*

"Through others, we become ourselves."

—Lev Vygotsky (1989, p. 56)

A student hears from a few of his classmates that they are going to create a movie for a class project. He asks his teacher about the project, telling her he wants to be a filmmaker one day and values this work. The teacher, however, chose students based on their ability levels and history of completing assignments ahead of their classmates and answers, "I have a different project chosen for each of you. The assignment you will be doing is creating a poster."

The teacher failed to see the spark that could have engaged this student, focusing instead on the amount of time this student typically took to complete his assignments, which she perceived as a function of his ability. She had a preconceived idea that fast equated with smart. The message internalized by the student was clear: he isn't smart enough to take on a creative assignment or collaborate with other students. A few words can repress an ambition or change a life.

Words can be simple, yet their effects are complex. Author Peter Johnston (2012) reminds us that "a single comment can profoundly change the academic and moral choices children make. It literally changes the world they live in" (p. 13). The words we choose can ignite or suppress an idea, initiate or deter an action, or inspire or hinder a mind. We are responsible for our word choices. We have the power to fuel minds or break spirits often just by the words we use. This chapter is about the surprising ways words we use can ignite or extinguish each child's passion for learning.

INTERNAL DIALOGUE

Figure 4.1 emphasizes internal dialogue. Internal dialogue is the discussion that occurs in your head regarding the thoughts and feelings of your experiences. This internal, constant conversation can change the way people perceive themselves and the world around them. The world, as a whole, is filled with negative messages that impact people, including words that create an uncaring culture. The following are sample messages that result in destructive internal dialogue:

Figure 4.1   Internal Dialogue—"I Think"

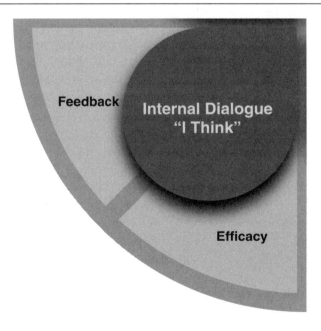

Figure 4.2   Efficacy and Feedback Defined

Term	Definition
Efficacy	Belief in one's ability to accomplish a task
Feedback	"Information provided by an agent (e.g., teacher, peer, book, parent, self, experience) regarding aspects of one's performance or understanding" (Hattie & Timperley, 2007, p. 81)

- Asking questions that make students feel defensive
- Words that don't show empathy to the root cause of a student's situation
- Using an aggressive tone in your words
- Using words that demonstrate your disinterest in the student's voice

To combat negative messaging, we need to make the choice to change students' internal dialogues. Students are then more likely to internalize their strengths, allowing them to reach their full potential. Positive internal dialogue brings out abilities in students in ways that help them think differently, with statements such as "I think that I am headed in the right direction in my learning," "I think positively about myself as a learner," and "I think I can accomplish the tasks important to my learning."

USING POSITIVE SUPPOSITIONS TO INFLUENCE STUDENTS' VIEWS OF THEMSELVES AND TRANSLATE TO CONFIDENCE IN THE CLASSROOM

Positive suppositions are when we assume positive intent in everything about people and situations. The story at the beginning of this chapter is a clear example of the absence of positive suppositions and the tragic effect it had on one learner. The influence of positive suppositions on feedback affects a learner's internal dialogue. Cultures of learning are built on the positive suppositions that we all have areas of expertise and that every member of our community of learners adds value to our classroom. Teachers who voice positive suppositions and model high expectations help students develop the capacity to realize their full potential. Using positive language, teachers help students identify their strengths and reinforce constructive internal thoughts about their abilities. A teacher who uses language that affirms students' potential to achieve their goals will be perceived as allies—who believes in students and will not give up on them when they take a risk and fail.

Not only do the words we use matter, but the context in which we use them is equally important. "Nice job" can mean one thing from a trusted friend and something entirely different from a sarcastic critic.

Vygotsky recognized the importance of social environment and how people assimilate language and experience through social interaction. Vygotsky (1978) says language and thoughts are inter-related; through language, we clarify ideas and solidify thinking.

Yeager and colleagues (2013) found that using positive feedback with students, letting them know that the feedback was based on high expectations, and ensuring students of the teacher's faith in students' abilities to reach those expectations caused students to revise their papers and improve their performance at significantly higher rates than students who didn't have access to these supports.

Reflect on a time when someone spoke negatively to you.

How did those words influence the choices you made?
How did what was said affect how you think about yourself?

You might have been able to hear the words and move on, or you might have internalized them.
Reflect on a time when someone said something positive to you.

How did those words influence the choices you made?
How did what was said affect how you think about yourself?

Consider a teacher giving feedback to a student about two paragraphs the child has written. The following examples (Figure 4.3) illustrate how words can affect how a student perceives what is important for him- or herself.

Figure 4.3   Feedback Examples

The teacher reads the work, comments, "Nice handwriting, but you need to correct your spelling," and then leaves to meet with another student. The student writer receives the message that presentation is more important than content.	A more effective message is to comment on the voice, word choice, or ideas in the two paragraphs and then ask a question to get the student to delve deeper into his or her writing. Some comments might be: "Wow! Your description of the cat 'moving like a shadow and the only hint of knowing the cat was there was the glow of its eyes,' drew me in as a reader. One thing I wondered about was how the character in the story reacted when the boxes tipped over. Can you tell me more about that? I think that if you work these details together, the story will be even better.'" In this way, the writer gets feedback on what he or she is doing well and scaffolding on how to improve.

This teacher, being knowledgeable about positive suppositions, has influenced the student's self-identity.

Peter Johnston, Haley Woodside-Jiron, and Jeni Day (2001) studied the effects of teacher's language on students in their article "Teaching and Learning Literate Epistemologies." In a summary of an interview, a young student shared her thoughts on literacy. The student said good readers are those who are quiet and read chapter books. This child identified quiet behavior with being a good reader. Some students, however, comprehend material better when they read aloud or ask questions. If a student who needs to read aloud or discuss the material in order to comprehend receives the message that quiet equals good, that child may identify him- or herself as a poor learner. The quoted student also said good readers read chapter books. In this case, the teacher inadvertently may have transmitted the message that chapter books are more valued than other texts even though some picture books have richer vocabulary or deeper meaning than some chapter books. Students who are reading nonfiction, poetry, or picture books would get the wrong message (Johnston et al., 2001).

The student also said that she does not help other students in the classroom because that "would be giving them things that you thought of in your head" (Johnston et al., 2001, p. 11). The teacher has fostered an environment through her words and actions that leads students to believe that they must come up with answers on their own and that cooperative working is not valued. The student said she does not help others because she sees that her ideas as something she should keep and that sharing ideas is a form of cheating. Research underscores the need for adults working with students to be mindful of the impact of their language on the students they teach (Johnston, 2004).

How would this scenario change if the teacher's daily talk included phrases such as "Find a partner, and for one minute and 40 seconds, share how you believe the character from our read-aloud will react to the encounter with the school bully?" Or, "We are fortunate to have a class of students who all think differently. When I am stuck, I find it useful sometimes to talk with another student who might help me see a problem from a different viewpoint." These positive suppositions on the part of the students frame the classroom as a place where other students' thoughts and ideas are valued, and thinking grows as students collaborate. Through intentional language, we help develop students' mindsets.

DEVELOPING STUDENTS' INTERNAL DIALOGUE BY USING LANGUAGE INTENTIONALLY

Students are influenced by isolated and accumulated interactions. Using supportive language and reflective questions can empower, while telling the child what to do or not do the next time a similar situation arises can cause them to avoid taking risks.

Suppose a child reaches for something and tips over a glass container by mistake. Adults might have different responses.

Reaction 1: Get away from that, sit on a chair, and think about what you have done.

Reaction 2: We need to clean this up, so no one gets hurt. I saw you reaching in the cupboard for an item and accidentally knocked the glass over. What might you do in the future?

The first reaction communicates that mistakes are not tolerated. The child is isolated and told to be passive after taking a risk to perform a task independently. Might the language cause risk aversion? Might the language impair future learning?

Have our words and actions as teachers created the conditions that engage our students in learning or shut them down? How do our reactions, words, and questions cause students to change their mindsets?

In the second reaction, the word *we* is deliberate, signifying that together, as a team, the adult and the child will clean up the mess. It conveys to the child that mistakes happen and that we are responsible for cleaning them up and learning from them—an approach that fosters independence.

Our last section of Chapter 4 focuses on feedback. We are introducing the conversation around choice words (Johnston, 2004) first so that the feedback discussion is more informed and meaningful. Carol Dweck (2006), a Stanford psychology professor, has studied student learning growth and attributes achievement to moving from a fixed mindset to a growth mindset. Students with fixed mindsets view intelligence as an inborn trait. Students with growth mindsets believe they develop their intelligence through their own effort. A number of studies (Craven, Marsh, & Debus, 1991; Dweck, 2000, 2006; Johnston, et al., 2001) support the argument that the language adults and students use can affect a student's mindset. For example, when young children are told they are smart, they are more likely to avoid risk when they encounter challenging materials. Students who believe that intelligence is based on effort work to improve and overcome obstacles, and they take on more challenging assignments.

Students come to school with growth or fixed mindsets and react to their environments accordingly. Some have growth mindsets and will persevere when confronted with difficulty. Teachers must help reengage students with fixed mindsets.

Michelle, a quiet first grader, transferred from another school, struggled greatly in the early months. The teachers heard Michelle making negative comments about her abilities, such as,

"I can't learn this like the other kids because I'm not smart enough." By listening closely to Michelle, her teachers discovered that her kindergarten teacher had frequently remarked to Michelle and her mother that Michelle's learning abilities were limited.

The staff at Michelle's new school took personal responsibility for her learning and regularly communicated to her that they believed she was capable of meeting challenges. She trusted them and felt that she could count on each of them to help. Teachers taught Michelle strategies to help her make gains in reading and math. Each day, teachers asked inquiry questions and encouraged Michelle to reflect on how she came up with answers. Rather than praising her intelligence, they praised her ability to learn different strategies that allowed her to solve many different types of problems. Teachers frequently commented on how much effort she put forth and how much these efforts were paying off. She was often reminded that the brain, like a muscle, could be developed by exercising it. By the end of first semester, Michelle was catching up to her peers, and by the end of the year, she regularly collaborated with peers and felt like an equal. Michelle told the adults in her school that she aspired to become a teacher when she grew up, so she could help children in the same way that she was helped.

Michelle's success can be attributed to a combination of nurturing relationships, receiving positive messages, stimulating inquiry through feedback, a growth mindset, and perseverance. Michelle connected her learning to new strategies rather than innate ability. Michelle was fortunate to have teachers who understood the power of forming a growth mindset.

In contrast, Elaine came into a classroom after first quarter. Her parents said they were moving her because her last teacher could not meet her needs because she was gifted and reading well beyond grade level. The first words Elaine spoke to her new teacher upon entering the classroom were these: "I am one of the smartest kids in my school." The teacher soon found that Elaine did have strong strategies in reading and math; however, she also was afraid to try new challenges.

Elaine had a positive image of herself as smart but with a fixed mindset. A fixed mindset, even if it is with an image of being smart, is a liability because it manifests itself in avoiding challenges and never acknowledging the need for high effort. In order to combat the fixed mindset, the teacher told students each one had unique gifts and that each person in the class could learn from the others. She taught lessons on how challenging projects could help build new neurons in the brain. Elaine was encouraged to grow new dendrites by applying herself through tasks that were difficult for her. She was told that struggling was part of the process of creating new pathways in her brain. Through the support of ongoing messaging, Elaine felt safe to begin to take risks and viewed herself differently as a learner.

Some educators may succumb to believing in a fixed mindset, leading to self-fulfilling prophecies for the students they work with. If students receive messages about their lack of ability in a content or skill area, they can take on the teacher's fixed mindset and carry this belief with them throughout their lives. Educators who help students focus on growth opportunities change students' inner dialogues so that they begin to think, "I can't do this yet, but with more effort, I will get better at it."

In many cases, a student is influenced by the mindset modeled by adults. Brendgen, Wanner, Vitaro, Bukowski, and Tremblay (2007) studied how students who received negative messages from their teachers in the primary grades suffered adverse effects throughout school. They found girls were the most affected, with their chances of high school graduation dropping by 7 percent. Licht and Dweck (1984) also studied primary-age children and found that students who showed helpless responses when presented with challenges most likely had heard critical or disciplinary comments from adults. If the adult is punitive in nature, the student will take on a fixed mindset. Conversely, if the adult with a growth mindset mimicked adults offering encouraging words and comments relating to effort, students would be more likely to take on a growth mindset.

EFFICACY THROUGH DELIBERATE LANGUAGE

Efficacy is the belief in one's ability to accomplish a task. When you ask an adult if a teacher ever made a difference in his or her life, the adult typically responds with a story. Consider the following story about Kelly's school experience.

Kelly thought she was an average student. Her best friend was a straight A student. Kelly assumed this was because her friend was just naturally smart. It was not until Kelly went into middle school that her sixth-grade language arts teacher saw characteristics in her that she had not seen in herself.

When Kelly presented a project in class, the teacher noticed that Kelly took great pains to make it informative and entertaining. He shared that he noticed Kelly using her artistic skills as well as her imagination to bring things to life and wondered what her creative mind would do the next time Kelly presented. This simple comment caused Kelly to see herself different, as capable. When he noticed that she shared her ideas with her peers to get ready for a presentation, he shared how he noticed her leadership skills. When Kelly didn't do well on a quiz, he shared that this was not like her and that he knew that on the next quiz she would do better. His comments began to change Kelly's internal dialogue. Her new thoughts were more like this: "I think of myself as creative, I think of myself as a leader, and I think of myself as capable." When a student believes in his- or herself as capable, a strong sense of efficacy emerges.

Directly related to internal dialogue is the self-talk of students. Self-talk focuses on the internal messages that a person says to him- or herself about his or her abilities. Kelly's self-talk of positive messages became the running commentary she began to tell herself about her abilities. Self-talk has positive effects on students' performance and self-confidence (Hatzigeorgiadis, Zourbanos, Mpoumpaki, & Theodorakis, 2008), and adults can affect directly the chances of positive self-talk. Several studies have found that positive statements made by teachers lead to increased positive self-talk in students (Burnett, 1999; Zourbanos, Hatzigeorgiadis, Tsiakaras, Chroni, & Theodorakis, 2010).

When students have positive internal dialogue, their efficacy increases as well (Schunk & Mullen, 2012). Acknowledging the mutual impact between both internal dialogue and efficacy leads to taking on a deeper meaning. Efficacy, much like growth mindset, allows students to feel as if they can take on difficult tasks as challenges rather than threats. "Self efficacy beliefs lead to greater persistence in the face of difficulties, reduce fear of failure, improve problem-focused analytical thinking and raise aspirations" (Bandura, 1995, p. 169). Albert Bandura, the psychologist and originator of social learning theory, states that efficacy needs to happen twofold, between students and teachers. Students with a high development of efficacy believe they can accomplish tasks, and teachers with high levels of efficacy believe they can truly make a difference in a student's accomplishments (Bandura, 1995). Therefore, to build efficacy, adults need to be mindful of the language they use. Through positive assumptions, choice words, self-efficacy, and feedback, teachers can support or inhibit student's internal dialogues. Similarly, administrators can support or inhibit staff's internal dialogue as well.

USING CAREFUL FEEDBACK TO AID IN STUDENTS' REFLECTION

In formative feedback, timing, specificity, and the quality of the dialogue all are important. An example would be the coach who, during a track meet, gives specific feedback to the runner such as, "Arms!" During practice, the coach helped the runner realize that when the runner made 90-degree angles in her arm swing, it opened up her stride to run faster. Because this was a new awareness that arose out of focus and concentrated effort in practice, the simple word *arms* helps the runner change her stride during the race. It was the timing as well as the specificity that helped the runner. A week prior, the coach sat down with the runner and shared her individual lap splits for each lap of the mile. Simply sharing the data and asking her, "What trends do you see in your lap splits?" was an example of formative feedback that caused the runner to reflect. The runner looked over the results and noted that it was the third lap that consistently was slower than the others. It just so happened that it was the third lap when the coach yelled, "Arms." This example illustrates the importance of timing, specificity, quality of the dialogue, and contemplation as important pieces of feedback.

Formative feedback is "information provided by an agent (e.g., teacher, peer, book, parent, self, experience) regarding aspects of one's performance or understanding" (Hattie & Timperley, 2007, p. 81). Formative assessment is the improvement vehicle, while feedback is what brings that vehicle to life. "It is important to be mindful to stage the classroom and instructional design so that feedback is maximized, instructional practices include intentional formative assessment and feedback leads to contemplation. Hattie (2009) indicates that intentional feedback can increase learning twofold. Teachers can apply a planned process to more quickly move students to the point of making their own adjustments. In *Transformative Assessment,* James Popham (2008) says teachers can use assessments to elicit evidence of students' understanding and then adjust their instruction, and students can adjust the strategies they have used. Both the teacher and the student intend to improve learning and actively engage in a known, planned process that leads to reflection and change. By educator's knowledge and action, the use of feedback can either accelerate or inhibit learning.

Effective teachers balance the tasks of affirming and supporting their students through giving them quality feedback that will empower students to adjust their learning. Educators play increasingly important roles in developing students' understanding a sense of self—personally, socially, and academically. Each is strengthened through intentional, quality feedback. Clearly, the words we choose to use and how we give that feedback can either support or inhibit student learning.

For example, a teacher is working with a student on a writing assignment. The student has written a story about her grandfather's life. The teacher will want to honor the student's feelings and may respond with a phrase such as, "I can see that your grandfather was very important to you by the memories you have of him. Can you tell me about why milking the cows with your grandfather stands out so clearly for you?" The student explains the event, and the teacher responds by stating, "If you write the words you just shared in your retelling, it will help the reader visualize this important moment." This balance between establishing interpersonal relationships and promoting academic achievement is an important area for educator reflection. Establishing caring relationships is the cornerstone of feedback that improves student engagement and is a requirement for igniting students' love of learning (Yeager et al., 2013).

Consider the impact of a personalized, reflective question that helps the student delve into her writing: "Here in your story, you shared that you and your grandfather harvested the corn together. What makes this such an important event for you in your relationship with your grandfather?" In contrast, what if the teacher responded, "I told you the paper needed to be a page, and you only wrote two paragraphs" as she handed the paper back to the student? The message in the first instance tells the writer the teacher has understood the feelings she has worked to evoke and wants to help her improve her expression. The message in the second case is that content is less important than the length of the paper, and absence of teacher attention to relationship was evident.

Various forms of feedback exist and are used commonly. Some of those forms of feedback are a far greater value to students stimulating their thinking. Understanding the need to move from evaluative to formative feedback will serve the teacher and student well. Figure 4.4 shows common statements and questions that teachers might use in the classroom that reflect a continuum of feedback. The comments are sorted into categories by types of statements.

The comments in the first three columns are evaluative. Judgment and personal observation statements may help a student comply in the moment yet do not help in the long term. Inference statements are what the teacher believes about a student. Students might feel good at that moment; however, these kinds of comments do not relate to a learning target or help students improve their learning. As we reflect on our current instructional practice, if a high percentage of our feedback mirrors the gray-shaded portion of the continuum in Figure 4.4, then we are falling short of preparing students with the self-reflection and higher-order skills to succeed in school, life, and work. Conversely, if a majority of our

Figure 4.4 Analysis of Feedback Continuum

Judgment	Personal Observation	Inference	Data	Inquiry
Very good. You did a great job! I don't think you put in any effort into that project.	I like the way you are sitting. I like how quietly you are speaking. I enjoyed hearing your story.	You are respectful. You are good at math. You really thought hard about that.	Here you are talking about . . . and then you jump to . . . You completed two entries in your journal.	Here you are talking about . . . and then you jump to . . . Does that flow in your story? What strategies did you use to solve that?

Source: Modified from Costa and Garmston (2005).

feedback resides in the data and inquiry, we can be confident that our students are changing their internal dialogue as a result of metacognition. If our practice is in the first three columns, then the goal should be to shift current practice to inquiry.

In the data and inquiry columns, the teacher facilitates, so students are empowered to reflect on their learning. This helps students internalize the data and move into higher levels of thinking by having students analyze or evaluate their thinking. Teachers' instructional practice is influenced through intentionality around their analysis of their feedback.

In order to meet rigorous, high standards that emphasize higher-order thinking and problem-solving skills, educators will need to reexamine their instructional strategies to help students meet rigorous standards. Asking reflective inquiry questions gets students thinking in reflective and inquiry terms that will help them improve as learners and aligns with the standards' requirement for critical thinking.

VALUING STUDENT VOICE IN FEEDBACK

The questions teachers ask are key to the expectation that all students be lifelong learners. An especially powerful question is: "What questions do you have?" The way this question is being asked conveys the message that inquiry is a natural part of life. Harvey and Goudvis (2007) have observed that students can create thin or thick questions. Thin questions begin with *who, what,* and *where,* while thick questions are the *how* and *why* questions that help us delve into ideas more deeply. Questioning students in this manner also creates the ideal conditions where student voice is valued (Quaglia & Corso, 2014), increasing the probability of student engagement.

Another example of valuing voice comes from one teacher we know who posted a board outside of his classroom with a list of student-generated questions to help students with topics they were exploring and had questions about. While some students read and researched, other students, staff members, and parents wrote their contact information or other insights in response. The board helped students gather information and tap into the talents of those around them. Imagine the engagement in having the students joining in this activity as a collective support through technology.

When we focus our students on asking higher-level questions, we help develop their critical thinking abilities and as well as strengthen their voices. Peter Johnston (2004) uses the question "What problems did you come across today?" (p. 32) to reinforce the idea that all of us must solve problems each and every day. The ability to identify the problem and work toward its solution moves learners forward.

FORMATIVE ASSESSMENT AND FORMATIVE FEEDBACK STRATEGIES

Teachers may plan lessons in which formative assessments occur in the middle or at the end of the lesson in order to gauge students' levels of understanding and signal the need to adjust instruction. Teachers also may plan lessons that intentionally emphasize daily formative feedback. The assessment can be as simple as asking a question and having the students give a thumbs-up or thumbs-down or a fist-a-five, in which the students indicate their levels of understanding on a scale where a fist is zero understanding to five extended fingers representing full understanding. Teachers respond to students who say they don't understand by thinking of a new way to teach the concept. Some elementary teachers give each student a red and a green square paper. Students put a red square on their desks when they are confused, and the teacher knows to stop or slow down.

Some teachers identify students who may need additional support. During the lesson, the teacher walks around the classroom with a clipboard or iPad and makes notes of where each student is with respect to acquiring the skill to gauge which students need additional help. Another popular strategy is to require that students complete exit slips at the end of the period. Students complete exit slips by writing or illustrating their understanding of a concept. For example, fifth graders studying algebra are asked at the end of class to explain or draw a picture of a strategy to solve for x in the equation $2x + 9 = 6x$. They may write it out.

This exercise helps solidify students' understanding and gives teachers feedback about students' understanding. This approach also can help teachers communicate with families about the strategies students are learning.

Just as teachers learn to reflect and to adjust their instruction in response to formative assessment data, students should learn how to receive and interpret feedback, how to use that feedback to become better learners, how to make adjustments and self-correct, and to appreciate the importance of the process of learner

Figure 4.5   Algebra Exit Slip Example

Students who learned a new strategy in algebra may choose to share their learning through a representation such as this.

$$2x + 9 = 6x + 1$$
$$xx + 9 = xxxxxx + 1$$
$$9 = xxxx + 1$$
$$- 1 \qquad - 1$$
$$8 = xxxx$$
$$2 = x$$

adjustments. We become lifelong learners through mastering this cycle of self-assessment, reflection, and self-correction. Pete Hall and Alisa Simeral (2008) posit that the highest form of teacher effectiveness is the refinement stage at which teachers continually reflect. Similarly, student self-reflection is the first step to becoming an independent learner and a precursor to mastering the ability to make effective adjustments in their own learner processes.

A simple but powerful strategy for using feedback is to ask students to place two different colored sticky notes on their assignments. One color signifies a success, the other an area to improve. The student lists successes on one sticky note, such as rereading a portion of text and achieving a new level of understanding or successfully applying a study tip learned in class. The second note is used to flag an area of work that the student wishes to improve, such as a part of a story where the student is intending to create an effective thesis, but the student is seeking additional support in developing the idea. The sticky note tool can help a teacher quickly identify students' understanding and application and detect who may need a personal conference or re-teaching.

WHEN STUDENTS SELF-CORRECT

To influence students' internal dialogue, owning the responsibility to self-correct is an essential student action. Students can make adjustments during regular, daily lessons. Teachers can facilitate by sharing the goal of the day's lesson and clear expectations. Teachers may model or share examples of proficient and advanced work, or they may use class time to model and give students opportunities to practice assessing their own work by rating it on an agreed-upon rubric. The rubric will help students know their strong points as well as aspects of their performance that still need work.

For example, one student was given rubrics in all of his subject areas and asked to reflect on his year in third grade. The student recognized that learning math involved making his thinking visible by verbalizing or writing down the strategies he used to solve various problems. He also had to use math language to communicate and use tables, charts, or illustrations to share his mathematical reasoning. In the first quarter, the teacher asked the class to rate the mathematical thinking process of problems gathered from previous years (no names, of course) as well as practicing applying the skill to problems they were given. The student shared one day in class how he used the table he drew to explain his reasoning and figured out on his own that his approach to problem solving wasn't correct because the table allowed him to see his mistake. He was able to reflect and self-correct. When our feedback specifically gives students the strategies, tools, and encouragement, as well as time to practice implementing them successfully, it can improve their reflective processing and ability to self-correct.

Some school activities lend themselves easily to self-correcting, such as sports and performance arts including band and drama. However, with reflection and practice, we can also identify comparable opportunities in a classroom where performance, products, and projects are central to the learning. For example, in geometry, students are squaring up a potential building using the Pythagorean theorem $(A^2 + B^2 = C^2)$. In approaching the project, the student must understand the goal (squaring the building), understand the formula, and be trained to ask him- or herself essential questions:

- Why does a building have to be square? How do I adjust if it is not?
- If $A^2 + B^2$ isn't equaling C^2, what must I do to rework this problem to get it correct? The student would check his or her multiplication and self-correct the work.
- What adjustments in my computation on my part will cause me to square this foundation correctly?

When self-correcting becomes commonplace in the classroom, and teachers are skilled at monitoring the degree to which students understand, learning occurs at a higher level.

Teachers could have brief, one-on-one conferences about an essential question with the student to help gradually release the responsibility to the student so that he or she can work independently. When students áre habitually reflecting and self-correcting, they become intentional in framing their learning and monitoring their progress.

Becoming self-correcting learners assumes that students are able to reflect and focus efforts on learning. Believing that students have the ability to take ownership of their learning can become a self-fulfilling prophecy.

Our identities are molded through the words we hear to describe our actions. Words and the unspoken messages we receive inform our self-concepts and willingness to take risks as learners. Educators' words and actions have the power to help students take ownership of their learning and become their personal best.

TAKING ACTION

When classrooms become places where students feel free to ask questions and learners support one another, we create a space where taking a risk for learning is both natural and celebrated.

- Consider what actions you will take to bring awareness to the words used in the classroom and in homes.
- Begin with personal reflection. Some teachers videotape themselves in their classrooms and analyze their word choices.
- How often do you ask and use student feedback?

THE IMPLICATIONS OF INTERNAL DIALOGUE FOR EMOTIONAL, BEHAVIORAL, AND COGNITIVE ENGAGEMENT

Emotional, behavioral, and cognitive engagement are the result of internal dialogue. The language educators, staff, and students use, as well as the student's existing internal dialogue, creates an identity for the student that influences emotional engagement. Feedback that focuses on students' efforts instead of students' abilities positively affects emotional engagement. Educators must be mindful in building a culture where students are respectful of one another, creating a true community of support.

The language utilized in feedback also affects students' behavioral engagement, either helping or hurting. A culture of mutual support and growth among all stakeholders is fostered through respectful feedback, which creates an environment where we are happy for one another's success.

Positive internal dialogue is critical in creating the conditions in which cognitive engagement can flourish. Internal dialogue encompasses creating a safe environment where students can discuss, question, debate, and critique in order to grow as learners. Positive dialogue also invites student metacognition that allows them to think about their thinking, creating space for additional, positive self-talk.

INTERNAL DIALOGUE DISPOSITIONS

Once students have an understanding of growth mindset, they will be more open to feedback and have more self-efficacy. Take, for example, Gloria. She had learned about growth and fixed mindsets from her teacher and also spent time reflecting on herself with the use of an effort rubric that Carol Dweck created as part of Mindset Works. Gloria talked about areas of her life where she had a growth mindset and areas of her life when she was more fixed. She realized that she took on challenges, accepted feedback, and persevered in her music and sports but didn't feel the same way when it came to writing and math. It was at this point that the teacher was able to share strategies of self-talk in order to develop Gloria's mindset.

In the weeks following this learning, Gloria began to perceive feedback as helpful instead of judgmental, and she began believing that she could do better if she put forward the necessary effort. It was at this point that her teacher could see that Gloria and her classmates were ready to learn a set of dispositions in the arena of internal dialogue.

The dispositions under feedback are contemplation, open-mindedness, collaboration, and metacognition, which allow students to reflect deeply about their perceptions of learning and

Figure 4.6 Internal Disposition Through the Teacher's Eyes

Skills and dispositions to support key components of feedback	Students with internal dialogues internalize their strengths to reach their full potential. Students use self-talk to direct their thoughts into positive messages about self.		
"I think deeply about new ideas"	Skills/ Dispositions	Defined as	Supported by teachers who . . .
	Contemplative "I think deeply"	A deep, reflective thought	. . . give time for students to focus on a thought. This can happen by giving time for a student to journal or write or using a protocol where a student listens deeply to what another student is sharing without speaking or only asking questions about the topic the student is speaking about.
			. . . give students time to explore art, music, and dance or give students opportunities to volunteer.
	Open-Minded "I think about new ideas"	A willingness to listen and consider new ideas (Russell, 1939)	. . . model by treating opinions differently than one's own with respect.
			. . . use books where characters need to listen and see a new point of view such as *Duck, Rabbit, The Blind Man and the Elephant, Black and White,* and *The Cotton Quilt* (www.bestchildren'sbooks.org).
			A group of researchers found that using books where the students identified with the main characters helped students have fewer stigmatizations of groups or issues in real life (Vezzali, Stathi, Giovannini, Capozza, & Trifiletti, 2014).

Collaborative "I think two heads are better than one"	Working, thinking, and relating with others to achieve a shared goal (Dooly, 2008)	… help students set norms. … use protocols to help students practice the art of listening and paraphrasing what they hear. … teach students how to ask questions (Abler, 2012).
Metacognitive "I think about what I'm thinking about"	"The ability of the mind to monitor and redirect the activities of the brain, to plan a strategy for producing what information is needed, to be conscious of our own steps and strategies during the act of problem solving, and to reflect on and evaluate the productiveness of our own thinking (Costa & Kallick, 2014; Dunlosky & Metcalf, 2009; Hacker, Dunlosky, & Graesser, 2009)	… give time during class to self-reflect on progress, process, and thinking (Costa & Kallick, 2008) … use the phrases *Before I thought…Now I think…* or *How is my thinking changing?*

(Continued)

Figure 4.6 (Continued)

Skills and dispositions to support key components of self-efficacy **"I think positively about my abilities to succeed"**	Skills/ Dispositions	Defined as	Supported by teachers who . . .
	Optimistic "I think things will work out"	The ability to view life's situations through a lens of hopefulness and the belief in positive outcomes	. . . change mindset by having students practice positive self-talk. If a student seems to voice powerlessness in a situation, ask, "What efforts can you make to change the outcome of their situation" (Seligman, Revich, Jaycox, & Gilham 2007)?
	Agile "I think on my feet"	The ability to develop a new way of thinking and doing things	. . . ask students to share how they solve problems, highlighting that there is more than one way to solve a problem. Koutstaal (2012) states that to build agility in the mind means to give students time to pay attention to their environment and to incubate thoughts.
	Critical Thinker "I think about the logic and reasoning of ideas and conclusions"	The ability to engage in reflective, rational, and disciplined thinking to interpret, analyze, infer, and evaluate current thought (Scriven & Paul, 1987)	. . . give time and space for students to brainstorm, problem solve, test plans, and give options. Willingham (2007) cautions that in order for students to critically think about an idea, they must have the background knowledge and practice to think about it in critical ways.
	Confident "I think if I put my mind to this, I can be successful"	The belief in one's ability to do well or succeed at something	. . . encourage repeated attempts to try tasks. . . . teach coping behaviors. . . . scaffold challenges appropriately.

understand other people's views. Each of these dispositions will support students in working with others in the future.

Optimism, agility, critical thinking, and confidence fall under the umbrella of self-efficacy. Self-efficacy opens up the avenue for students to commit to their learning and meet personal goals. The students use these skills and dispositions to develop their internal voices, lay out learning strategies to complete tasks, and attribute failure to things in their own control so that they can meet goals.

Figure 4.8 can be used with students so that students can self-reflect on their current status within the internal dialogue continuum, including feedback and efficacy.

HOW INTERNAL DIALOGUE SUPPORTS PASSIONATE LEARNERS

Most educators enter the profession believing they will make a difference in students' lives. We build relationships and pinpoint students' strengths. We understand that our role is to feed students' natural curiosity and to inspire lifelong learning.

Figure 4.7   Internal Dialogue—"I Think"

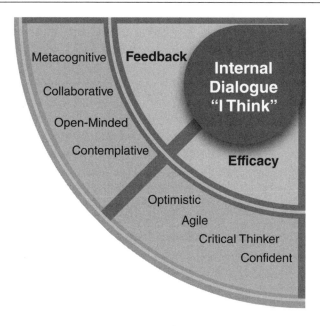

Figure 4.8 Internal Conditions of Feedback and Efficacy That Result in Passionate Learning

| | FEEDBACK | | | |
	Indifferent	Compliant	Engaged	Passionate
Contemplation	I think of myself as not capable of original thoughts.	I think about possible opportunities when asked to do so.	I think about the possible opportunities and outcomes of strategies.	I think about quality feedback that I am given and am thoughtful in the feedback I give myself and others in order to improve. I approach learning with contemplation, an open mind, a collaborative spirit, and time to reflect through metacognition.
Open-Minded	I think the ideas I have are really good and do not value other people's ideas.	I think about possible new ideas if an adult asks me to do so.	I think about the possibilities of new ideas.	
Collaboration	I think there is not much to gain by working with others.	I think that working alone works well for me, but I will work with others if asked to do so.	I think that by working with others, I can do better work.	
Metacognition	I think that I learn best when dealing with isolated concepts and prefer rote memorization.	I think that the work I complete is fine, and once I hand it in, I feel that I don't have to think any more about the assignment.	I think and reflect about my thinking and the strategies I use to problem solve.	

Internal Conditions That Result in Passionate Learning

	Indifferent	Compliant	Engaged	Passionate
			EFFICACY	
Optimism	I think that things are not going to go well. I struggle to see a positive outcome.	I think negative thoughts but vocalize what I think will please the teacher.	I think in positive ways and see the glass as half full.	I think positive messages about my learning and myself. Through positive self-talk, I take on difficult tasks as new challenges. I approach learning with optimism, agility, critical thinking, and confidence.
Agility	I think that my ideas are fine the way they are.	I think that my best work is when I follow directions and do the work like the teacher asks me to do it.	I think in terms of developing new ways of thinking and doing things.	
Critical Thinking	I think best with facts and memorization.	I think my learning is fine; however, if asked, I will try to use the strategies of analyze, infer, and evaluate.	I think about increasing my understanding by using the strategies of interpret, analyze, infer, and evaluate.	
Confidence	I think I do not have capabilities like others. I think of strategies to cover for my lack of confidence.	I think I can do what is necessary to do well.	I think of myself as being able to succeed.	

85

In the time teachers spend with students, they have hundreds of interactions, try numerous strategies, and speak countless words. Combined, these actions influence students' internal dialogues, all necessary in creating passionate learners.

The most effective teachers believe the culminating effect of these interactions, strategies, words, and time will help students adjust their views of learning so that they engage in inquiry, believe in perseverance, and shift to a growth mindset. Both teachers and students make these adjustments, although early adjustments may be more on the teacher's part. The combined effect over time of interactions, strategies, and words will result in students adjusting their learning strategies and processes. Students need time to develop more positive self-images as learners and to develop the capacity for risk taking.

As educators embrace the power that words have with students, we embark on an important journey to change not only students' mindsets but also the paths they will take in life. Children build their identities, learn what it means to work cooperatively with others, and find the talents in those they work with through words. Words not only change the culture of the classroom but also can reengage learners, eventually changing the world.

CHAPTER 5

Self–
Determination

$\mathcal{C}$ lassrooms across the United States have implemented a Genius Hour. Genius Hour is an idea inspired and made popular by Google's 20 percent time, where employees are able to use a day a week to work on an idea that could benefit the company. In schools, Genius Hour gives students a period a week to explore a topic they are passionate about to make a difference in their school, community, or world. It has allowed students to use their creativity while reigniting their excitement about learning as they research, interview, and enact their projects. At the same time, it allows teachers to connect with their students to understand what topics are of interest to them.

The key to Genius Hour is that students are able to determine, for themselves, the pathway they will take and the processes they will utilize to elicit new learning. Typically, when a "good student" is asked what he or she will do today, they provide a litany of what others have told them to do: "I will listen, I will follow directions, and I will do my homework as assigned." Genius Hour works because students can answer the I-will question for themselves.

Self is "the set of beliefs that teachers and students have about their capacity to be effective" (Frontier & Rickabaugh, 2014, p. 122). Self allows people to regulate their processes while trying out new experiences yet is grounded in what is motivating to the individual (Deci & Ryan, 1991; Reeve, 2006) while considering self and, in turn, self-determination. To support passionate learning, one must consider the opportunity students have to chart their own course for learning.

SELF-DETERMINATION THEORY

Self-determination theory supports the claim that people are most productive when they can make decisions centered on preferences and that meet their psychological and intrinsic needs (Ryan & Deci, 2000). When students are able to create their own goals and

Figure 5.1   Self-Determination—"I Will"

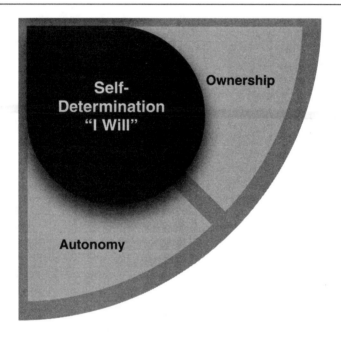

Figure 5.2   Ownership and Autonomy Defined

Term	Definition
Ownership	Empowering learners to make learning meaningful
Autonomy	The freedom of the learner to drive his or her actions (Deci & Ryan, 2000)

self-direct their learning, they naturally feel more ownership and invest deeper in their learning. Center stage in self-determination is the need for autonomy. Autonomy is the freedom learners have to determine their own actions. If students are involved in a classroom activity, perceive choice, are intrinsically motivated, and feel they have a sense of autonomy, then they feel a deeper ownership of their learning. Think about your own experiences in school or work when you were motivated and had established your own autonomy.

Don's oldest son provides a classic example of the components of self-determination theory being in place when he was five years old and in Montessori school. He became interested in the continents and the countries within these continents and decided to go about the process of learning the locations of hundreds of countries. He wasn't asked to learn the names and locations of the countries. His own self-fascination for learning's sake served as a driver for his extended engagement.

The research on autonomy support shows that students in classrooms with teachers who are more autonomy supportive than controlling are more engaged (Reeve, Jang, Carrell, Barch, & Jeon, 2004), have better academic performance (Boggiano, Fink, Shields, Seelbach, & Barett, 1993), are more likely to be persistent and stay in school (Vallerand, Fortier, & Guay, 1997), are more creative (Koestner, Ryan, Bernieri, & Holt, 1984), and have an overall better sense of well-being (Black & Deci, 2000). Autonomy-supportive teachers empower students to make choices whenever possible.

A teacher can be autonomy supportive by listening with interest and empathizing with the student. Students in classrooms with autonomy-supportive teachers are more likely than students with controlled teachers to show increased academic achievement, greater intrinsic motivation, and a desire to challenge self (Reeve, Bolt, & Cai, 1999; Shapira, 1976) as well as greater student engagement and positive academic attitudes (Pianta, Hamre, & Allen, 2011).

According to Reeve (2006), there are four key behaviors utilized by autonomy-supportive teachers: (1) Teachers look to students' interests and preferences; (2) teachers use informational, noncontrolling language; (3) teachers communicate why students are doing the activities they are involved in; and (4) teachers acknowledge and accept students' feelings and use their feedback to change their instruction. Each of the four behaviors will be expanded on next.

1. When teachers design their instruction with students' interests and preferences in mind, they acknowledge that all learning is personal. Examples of these behaviors include teachers who ask students to brainstorm specific ways that students might be able to reach a standard or include ideas from their interests to bring a concept alive. Many classrooms provide choice to help meet students' interests and preferences. This works well as long as students have clear goals and value the choice as important or interesting (Katz & Assor, 2007).

2. Informational and noncontrolling language allows the teacher to give specific and timely feedback to the learner after asking the student a question so that he or she can make an informed decision. In Chapter 4, we discussed the different levels of feedback. Understanding what we know about self-determination, ownership, and autonomy, it is clear that feedback focused on data and inquiry encourages learners to solve problems and revise work based on their own decisions rather than simply following the directives of the teacher. Perhaps for this reason, data and inquiry feedback is able to help students make a shift in the cognitive realm. In addition, informational feedback that is positive can make a significant impact on students' self-talk. Burnett (1999) found that teachers who made positive statements about students' abilities and efforts equated directly to students having positive self-talk and positive self-concepts of learning.

3. Communicating with students why they are doing an activity is a key concept for autonomy-supportive teachers and helps add value to the activity for the student. Without fail, there will be activities that students are not interested in. From the young student who is embarrassed to wear an oversized art shirt to protect his or her clothing during an art activity to a high school student who does not see the relevance of document-based questions (DBQs). When teachers are able to explain to the young child that the shirt is worn because the paint could permanently ruin an article of clothing, the child understands why he or she must wear the paint smock. When

the teacher explains that using a DBQ will help build confidence in analyzing a series of documents and aid in thinking skills to write a response to a historical question, the student will realize how this will help him or her decipher articles and learn at a deeper level. Thus, the students have motivation for enacting or learning about a particular topic and will feel less coerced into the activity (Assor, 2011). Teachers who are more autonomously supportive help explain to their students why they are partaking in an activity.

4. The final behavior utilized by autonomy-supportive teachers is the essence of effective teaching: acknowledging students' feelings about a topic and changing one's instruction based on student feedback. When one of the authors interviewed students about the learning process, a fourth-grade student shared the appreciation for a teacher by saying, "He will ask us about how he is teaching us, share what he wants us to understand or think, and he will ask us if we want to change anything about what he does. He gives us choices." Similarly, a high school student shared how his teacher "asks for student input and adjusts the pace of the class." He went on to say how difficult it is in other classrooms when someone or even the whole class doesn't get it, but the teacher continues to cover more of the curriculum. From a student's viewpoint, he or she is in school to learn. When a teacher ignores students' feelings and feedback, the students do not feel as if the teacher respects them as learners.

If teachers are consciously aware of being supportive of self-determination, then their classroom activities are consistent with students' needs and interests, which in turn, will contribute to students being involved in relevant activities that lead to motivated and engaged learners. One important point for teachers to understand is that a teacher who is more autonomy supportive is not synonymous with a teacher who promotes a lack of structure or a chaotic atmosphere. This is not autonomy supportive. Autonomy-supportive teachers adhere to rigorous expectations for quality learning but empower students to chart the path that will get them there. As John Hattie (2009) says, it is your agenda through students' eyes. In short, with too little structure and a laissez-faire classroom, students will not be fully engaged. Too much structure, and students can feel suffocated. As a quick guide, Figure 5.3 shares the differences between autonomy-supportive and controlling teachers. You can use this chart to assess if you are more autonomy supportive or controlling. It also can be used as a reference to expand your motivational style as a teacher if you are interested in becoming more autonomy supportive.

DIFFERENCES BETWEEN AUTONOMY SUPPORTIVE AND CONTROLLING TEACHERS

Figure 5.3   Differences Between Autonomy-Supportive and Controlling Teachers

What Do Autonomy-Supportive Teachers Do?	What Do Controlling Teachers Do?
Listen to what your students are sharing.	Ask students to listen to you.
Create opportunities for students to share ideas and discuss.	Create opportunities for students to get and give the right answer.
Teacher begins a unit by determining where students are in their understanding and sets goals with students to help them reach their goals. Students have control in their learning.	Teacher sets goals for whole class.
Environment is set up so that students are able to work in pairs or teams and have access to materials that will help them understand the concepts (e.g., math manipulatives).	Environment is set up so that students are able to watch or listen passively to the teacher.
Respond and adjust to students' questions and comments.	Counter students' comments with statements such as "Be more respectful" or "Change your attitude."
Use language that encourages effort and persistence.	Use controlling language to direct students.
Provide clear structure with choice and voice (encouragement).	Provide clear structure and directives (pressure and coercion).

THE IMPLICATIONS OF SELF-DETERMINATION FOR EMOTIONAL, BEHAVIORAL, AND COGNITIVE ENGAGEMENT

Self-determination as a form of intrinsic motivation directly links to the three realms of engagement: As teachers support an autonomy-supportive environment and understand what interests students have, the teacher is able to connect to students' emotional engagement. Students who feel that teachers know them well enough to be able to modify assignments or relate curriculum in a personal way have positive feelings about their classroom environment. In addition, self-determination gives voice to the students, and teachers who value students' thinking and feedback lead to supportive classroom communities.

Students who feel that their teachers are more autonomy supportive are more likely to exhibit signs of behavioral engagement. This is possible because self-determination moves away from a teacher-centered pedagogy to a student-centered pedagogy. Renzulli (2010) states that when students are at the center, driving instruction, it "focuses on the pursuit of real problems and should be viewed as the vehicle through which everything—from basic skills to advanced content and processes—comes together in the form of student-developed products and services" (p. 23). Self-determination allows students to have more autonomy and to give input on how learning will meet their interests, preferences, and needs. In addition, the way the teachers speak to the students, specifically through data and analysis feedback, shapes students' behavioral engagement. When teachers use phrases and questions that help students reflect, they are also giving students a sense of competence to think and solve problems. Students feel respected when they are listened to and feel they have some ability to control their learning. In addition, when teachers have high expectations for student learning, students rise to the challenge to meet the expectations of the teacher.

Self-determination has a direct impact on cognitive engagement as autonomous learners feel they have more flexibility and creativity in the classroom (Roth, Assor, Niemiec, Ryan, & Deci, 2009) and have increased achievement levels. When teachers support their students in tasks by challenging them or sparking their interest, they likely will inspire the students' intrinsic motivations (Pink, 2009), therefore engaging the students on a cognitive level.

SELF-DETERMINATION DISPOSITIONS

Students need ownership and a sense of autonomy in the classroom. This can be accomplished when students help set up classroom materials for easy access, are asked for their feedback in the learning process, and see the feedback being used in planning subsequent learning. In addition, the benefits are seen when teachers learn about students' interests so that they can make learning relevant to the students' lives and allow choice during collaboration and assignments. These classroom practices provide means for students to practice dispositions under self-determination.

SELF-DETERMINATION THROUGH THE TEACHER'S EYES

Students who have ownership of their learning will have natural opportunities to learn and practice the dispositions of inquisitiveness, emotionally invested, internalize, and transfer. When students have autonomy in the classroom, the environment is a place where students can learn and practice the dispositions of self-directed, self-control, self-monitoring, and self-starting, which help them practice the skills to grow in their abilities to be independent learners as seen in Figure 5.4.

HOW SELF-DETERMINATION SUPPORTS PASSIONATE LEARNERS

At the beginning of this chapter, the idea of Genius Hour was discussed. Genius Hour is an example of a curricular innovation that honors the components of self-determination in that students made decisions centered on what they were passionate about. When someone is passionate about an idea, he or she intrinsically is motivated to pursue, learn, and engage in the topic. Motivation is not something that gets done to people, rather it is something that people do. The question people need to ask is: "How can people create the conditions within which others will motivate themselves?" (Deci & Flaste, 1995, p. 10). The students' ownership in the project makes them invested in the final product, and students set goals accordingly. The students

Figure 5.4 Self-Determination Through the Teacher's Eyes

Skills and dispositions to support key components of ownership	Students with self-determination create their own goals and self-direct their learning. They feel more ownership and invest in their learning.		
"I will"	**Skills/Dispositions**	**Defined as**	**Supported by teachers who . . .**
	Inquisitiveness "I will ask when I wonder"	Desire to ask questions in order to learn more (Barell, 2003)	. . . model questioning, such as "I wonder why" or "What would happen if . . ." Give time for students to explore their answers. In the early grades, take an active role in helping the student find answers.
	Emotionally Invested "I will form relationships and express my feelings"	Process of investing in something or someone	. . . accept the students for who they are. If students feel that people are investing in them, they more likely will feel they can invest in someone or something. A simple guide is to show compassion and commitment to students and to continually communicate this with your students (Lacy, 2009).
	Internalize "I will carry this learning with me beyond school"	Process of integrating new information, values, beliefs, and opinions and embedding them into one's existing beliefs, attitudes, and values	. . . expects and shares high expectations. If a student doesn't share the high value or belief, the teacher needs to re-share the value or belief and ask questions of the students to understand their current beliefs. Individual conversations need to take place to help the students understand and determine the preferred value or belief (Yeager et al., 2013).
	Transfer "I will apply the skills to new situations"	Ability to take from one context and see a logical application to another context (Gage & Berliner, 1998)	. . . allow time for students to explore ideas and compare and contrast ideas related to previous ideas. Learners must be able to conceptualize a concept versus memorization or learning procedures. Gage and Berliner (1998) share the following questions to facilitate transfer: • How in this problem like others I have solved before? • Does anything here remind me of anything I have learned earlier? (Gage & Berliner, 1998, p. 301).

(Continued)

Figure 5.4 (Continued)

Skills and dispositions to support key components of autonomy **"I will"**	Skills/Dispositions	Defined as	Supported by teachers who . . .
	Self-Directed "I will set a course of action and follow it"	Ability to take initiative and responsibility to select, manage, and assess one's own learning (Gibbons, 2014)	. . . give time for students to set goals. . . . work as a facilitator for the learning process . . . teach students how to inquire, self-evaluate, and progress their work (Gibbons, 2014).
	Self-Control "I will choose my behavior to accomplish goals"	The ability to have self-discipline over one's body and mind (Baumeister & Tierney, 2011)	. . . provide an organized classroom environment and provide consistency. . . . model regulating emotions. Students need emotional support such as "affection, sensitivity to student's needs, and encouragement" versus "criticism, indifference to individual needs, and verbal control" (Willingham, 2011, p. 24).
	Self-Monitoring "I will think about where I am going, where I am, and what comes next"	Students assess themselves and record where they are in their learning process and evaluate themselves to a standard (Loftin, Gibb, & Skipa, 2005)	. . . enable students to use tools such as checklists, rating scales, rubrics, and matrixes to self-monitor their progress (Chafouleas, Riley-Tillman, & Sugai, 2007; Langford & Cleary, 1995).
	Self-Starting "I will allocate time and energy to achieve my goals"	Motivated to start an initiative on one's own	. . . begin with routines where students can initiate an activity or discussion as soon as they walk into the classroom. This is very different than taking a seat and waiting for the teacher to give direction. Also, ask students to do some planning on how they will complete an assignment.

Figure 5.5   Self-Determination—"I Will"

have the autonomy to drive their actions and find joy in pursuing the topic and engaging at more meaningful and deeper levels. As students wrestle and connect with new ideas, they reignite their excitement about learning. When the teacher learns more about what drives the students and is able to support them when challenges arise, the teacher is able to make deeper connections with the students and understand what support truly motivates them. Larry Page, the cofounder of Google, states that "my job as a leader is to make sure everybody in the company has great opportunities, and that they feel they're having a meaningful impact and are contributing to the good of society" (Lashinsky, 2012, para. 4). This is not unlike the experiences we want our students to experience. By using the four components of culture, mindset, internal dialogue, and self-determination, we will further engage students to become passionate learners. Figure 5.6 can be used with students so that they can self-reflect on their current status with self-determination including ownership and autonomy.

Figure 5.6 Internal Conditions of Ownership and Autonomy That Result in Passionate Learning

	OWNERSHIP			
	Indifferent	Compliant	Engaged	Passionate
Inquisitive	I will listen and learn the information that others have determined to be important.	I will come up with questions if my teacher asks me to.	I will ask questions to learn more.	I will make my learning more meaningful through empowering myself and taking ownership of my learning. I approach learning with an inquisitive mind, emotionally investing in the task and people, internalizing the learning, and transferring new information to other areas.
Emotionally Invested	I will be guarded against opening myself to someone or something.	I will focus on a task or person if asked to do so.	I will open myself by investing my time and energy into something or someone.	
Internalize	I will operate at the surface level on most everything.	I will reflect on what I believe about a new idea introduced if asked to do so.	I will seek out new ideas and beliefs and reflect on how they work in my own beliefs.	
Transfer	I will see what is present before me and not look beyond that.	I will think about how something can be applied to a new situation if asked to do so.	I will apply learning to new situations.	

AUTONOMY

	Indifferent	Compliant	Engaged	Passionate
Self-Directed	I will be OK if I have to be reminded or prodded to work on something.	I will follow the routines set up by my teacher.	I will initiate an activity on my own.	I will drive my action because I have autonomy. I approach learning through being able to self-direct my learning, self-control my body and mind, self-monitor my situation, and self-start my learning.
Self-Control	I will try to control my body and mind; however, I am easily taken off task and struggle to regroup.	I will follow the rules and routines set up by my teacher so that it looks like I am in control of my body and mind.	I will control my own body and mind.	
Self-Monitoring	I will try to reflect, but I do not have a habit of self-reflecting.	I will self-evaluate my progress when asked to do so.	I will evaluate how I am doing in my learning and reflect on my progress over time.	
Self-Starting	I will say that I will get started on something, but then I procrastinate, often letting issues build until I find myself in crisis.	I will take care to do the things that are assigned to me.	I will be motivated to start an initiative on my own.	

CHAPTER 6

Classroom Culture

Setting the Tone for Engagement

A robotics competition was being held at a local middle school. As parents slipped in and out of the classrooms watching teams compete in different events, one parent spent a little more time than the others observing what was on the walls in the rooms he visited. As much as he tried to leave his work at the office, his training as an anthropologist required him to make meaning from his surroundings. As he'd told his daughter enough times, everything in an environment tells a story about the values and beliefs of the people who control that environment.

He looked around the first classroom. He knew it was a math classroom only because there were three teachers' editions of math texts on the teacher's desk. Around the room were posters of famous tennis players, including a poster with a tennis ball going past a frustrated player's racquet that read, "That's the way the ball bounces." Next to the clock was a large sheet of poster paper; it read,

Rules of the Game:

Be in your seat with all work done and your textbook out BEFORE the bell rings.

Be quiet; other people are actually working.

If you have a question for me, raise your hand.

Don't bother others; listen the first time, and figure it out yourself.

Place the proper heading on top of your assignment: name, date, page number.

The official (me) will call a "Double Fault" if you fail to follow these rules twice. This will result in a loss of homework points, a "zero," or an office referral.

The official is always right.

Below this poster was another that read, "If you think it is odd that I only ask you to do the odds, you can do the evens too." The parent thought to himself, "This teacher really likes tennis, and I would have been given a lot of double faults when I was a kid." The parent walked into a second mathematics classroom. In this classroom, anchor charts with mathematical concepts, examples of student work, and student reflection statements about their progress were on the walls around the room. In the front of the room were sheets of paper with the prompt: *I get better at math when I . . .* followed by statements handwritten in black permanent marker, such as these: *Ask questions when I get stuck. Watch sample problems being solved on the Web! Practice my weaknesses.* Each was signed by a student. Over the whiteboard on a large sheet of poster paper, the teacher had written, "This is important. With effort we can do anything. I will never give up on you!" Her signature and a smiley face were written underneath. A second sheet of poster paper was next to the clock; it read "How We Will Support Our Learning" and was surrounded by student signatures:

1. We arrive ready to learn more and get even better.

2. We listen to others; there is a lot of knowledge in this room.

3. We have the courage to ask questions. Questions make everyone smarter.

4. We support each other using positive words and actions.

5. We read and follow directions for assignments.

6. We use our "I get better at math" strategies. If my strategy isn't working for me, I have permission to use someone else's.

7. We do these things because to build a new house, or design a better engine, or make money in finance, or grow more food on smaller plots of land, or design a new video game, or produce an awesome song, or buy a new phone, or finance a new Mustang, or plan a trip to climb Mt. Everest, or to cure cancer . . . we'll need math.

The parent thought to himself, "How can I get my kids in this classroom, and can I come too?"

It doesn't take an anthropologist to see the dramatic differences in these two classrooms. These two classrooms are in the same building. They serve the same board of education. They operate under the same policies. They are subject to the same politics. They teach to the same standards. The teachers, however, are operating under very different premises about the purpose of their classrooms and the level of commitment they expect from each learner. These different premises and purposes have resulted in two distinct and unique classroom cultures.

CULTURE DEFINED

Culture is the way things are done around here (Drucker, 2002). Like a fish unaware of water, we are typically not aware of culture until we visit an environment that is uniquely different from our own. We've had a chance to visit schools around the world. Across Asia, there is a clear cultural norm of respecting the hierarchy of leadership. Students stand when an adult enters the room. Teachers use formal titles when talking to the principal. Across Africa, students and teachers wear uniforms. Teachers wear a polo shirt bearing the school's colors and a white lab coat over the polo shirt. As an outsider, these are little things that we notice right away because they are so different from what we're accustomed to seeing in most schools in the United States.

As our father and anthropologist noted in the opening anecdote, classrooms have unique cultures as well. The assumptions

Figure 6.1   Culture—"We Are"

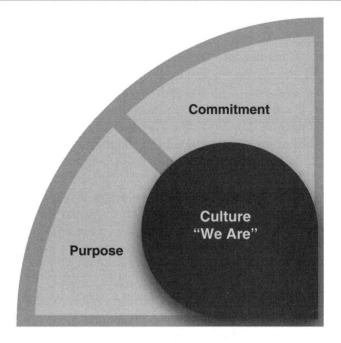

Figure 6.2   Purpose and Commitment Defined

Term	Definition
Purpose	Contribute to things greater than self (Pink, 2009)
Commitment	Dedication to task or learning (Pink, 2009)

of classroom culture are so ingrained in our perceptions of what school *is* that these expectations can be utilized for comic effect in television shows and movies about school. A marvelous example of this is the film *School of Rock*. Jack Black plays a slacker musician and an unqualified substitute teacher who is placed mistakenly in an elite prep school. He is shocked by the gap between how he thinks a classroom should be run and what students expect of him. There is an ongoing barrage of comments from students about how his approach to everything he does is not the way they usually do things around here. Beyond the humor that lies at the core of this disconnect in expectations of classroom culture, there are meaningful differences in the cultural norms of schools and classrooms that have a dramatic effect on students' learning environments.

In math classes the anthropologist described, for example, there will be marked differences in how the two classrooms engage in discussion. Over a period of weeks or months, the approach becomes a part of the classroom culture. *It is just how things are done in this classroom.* However, those routines started with a set of assumptions made by each teacher: a set of assumptions about whose voice is most important, whose voice should be heard, and the rules that must be in place for a discussion to occur successfully. Too often, we see classroom cultures that are predicated on efficiency and compliance. When establishing a culture focused on engaging students to create and support passionate learners, we argue that decisions about classroom culture should be driven by (1) building shared purpose and (2) a commitment to learning. This intentionality requires teachers to choose between some important, but rarely discussed, dichotomies that underlie many of the assumptions that are made about classroom culture. These dichotomies make a profound difference in how we support each student's needs for cognitive, emotional, and behavioral engagement and can support or deflate each child's passion for learning.

In the 21st century, teachers need to be critically attuned to the value they provide by creating a supportive learning environment by knowing each student and helping students work with one another. If teaching is viewed simply as giving the lesson, assigning the work, correcting the work, and giving a grade, then teachers have become an anachronism. There are tools on the Internet that can do that more efficiently. However, in a classroom filled with passionate learners, the teacher demonstrates enthusiasm for the content he or she is teaching as well as for the kids who are learning. He or she identifies each student's talents and strengths, celebrates accomplishments, encourages risk, provides challenge, and cheers students on to new levels of learning. Furthermore, the capacity of the students in the class does not go unrealized. Each student supports every other student's passion and commitment to think, grow, and achieve. In a culture that supports passionate learners, there is a commitment to each other. In a classroom of passionate learners, there is a sense of shared purpose. *We are here to learn. We are here to improve. We are here to support one another.*

Creating a classroom that has a culture conducive to creating and supporting passionate learners requires a shared purpose and a shared commitment to learning. A classroom that supports a shared purpose strives to create a culture where students contribute to things that are greater than self. A classroom that supports a commitment to learning strives to create a culture where students are dedicated to the tasks they are engaged in—and value the learning that results. For this to occur, teachers must make intentional choices about what will—and what will not—be valued in the classroom culture. Some of these values require an intentional shift away from anachronistic components that were of value in yesterday's classrooms but may be counterproductive for today's learners:

- A culture that supports passionate learners who are cognitively engaged is attuned to the distinction between . . .

  a performance environment as compared to a learning environment.

  a culture of answers versus a culture of inquiry.

- A culture that supports passionate learners who are emotionally engaged is attuned to the distinction between . . .

  a culture of judgment as compared to a culture of understanding.

  a culture of me as compared to a culture of we.

- A culture that supports passionate learners who are behaviorally engaged is attuned to the distinction between . . .

  a culture of compliance as compared to a culture of authenticity.

  a culture of low expectations versus a culture of high expectations.

Each of these dichotomies will be explored below to further clarify how school and classroom culture can develop shared purpose and shared commitments among teachers and learners to create the conditions for passionate learning.

A CULTURE OF PURPOSE AND COMMITMENT TO SUPPORT COGNITIVE ENGAGEMENT

A school and classroom culture that supports passionate learners values high levels of cognitive engagement. In these classrooms, students wrestle with challenging, authentic problems and see value in the better idea. A cognitively engaged student does not simply do his or her schoolwork to get it done; he or she is interested, even intrigued by the ideas and concepts that he or she is learning. We believe that cultures that support high levels of cognitive engagement are committed to establishing a *learning environment* rather than a *performance environment* in each classroom. Furthermore, these classrooms are driven to help students see that the purpose for engaging their work is best supported by a culture that values *inquiry* rather than a culture that merely values the right *answers*.

Cognitive Engagement as a Culture of Learning or a Culture of Performance?

Is the purpose of school learning or proving you are smart? We've asked this question of thousands of educators around the country, and time and again, we see clear patterns in responses. Typically, most teachers shake their heads and agree that their students would say *to prove you are smart.* Usually primary teachers are more likely to say the purpose is about learning, but we've heard many first-grade teachers talk about how they have students who "think they are dumb" or "are afraid to make mistakes." These responses are troubling. Untangling this problem requires us to create a distinction between a culture of learning and a culture of performance.

A culture of performance only values what is already known or what can already be accomplished. In this environment, nothing is formative; everything is summative; "I don't know" is not an acceptable answer. Everything counts, and everything counts against you. The assumption is that you should know this already. The risk of establishing a culture that always emphasizes performance is that *not knowing* is always perceived as a liability and is, therefore, avoided like the plague. Too often, unwittingly we can establish a classroom culture where we alienate students who have not already mastered the curriculum. For example, during the introduction of a unit, a teacher may ask a series of questions to the class that only a few students already know. The teacher asks the questions; those few students answer them. They are praised. The teacher assumes the other students know the answers as well and moves on to the next subject. Or, the students who do not know the answer internalize feelings of shame or doubt: *How did they know that? I must not be as smart as them.*

A culture of learning, on the other hand, values the development of new skills and understandings. The assumption in this culture is that the learner comes to the classroom with important skills and knowledge but has yet to learn a new set of skills and knowledge that will be built upon in this particular grade level or course. In a learning environment, it is OK to say, "I am confused," or "I have a question," or "I can't do this yet and need some help." Learning is rarely a linear process. It is a circuitous path of failure and success, confusion and clarity, and hopelessness and confidence. When students are in a classroom that values a culture of learning, they are free to acknowledge that there are skills and understandings that are currently beyond their grasp, but with time and effort, fluency and clarity will develop.

In their article clarifying the definitions of various types of achievement goals and their impact on student learning, Grant and Dweck (2003) distinguish between performance goals and learning goals. Performance or ability goals are pursued to demonstrate ability by (1) accomplishing a task or (2) avoid revealing a lack of ability by not engaging in a task. Conversely, learning, or mastery, goals are pursued to develop new knowledge or skills. While learning goal structures has been associated with student development (Cherepinsky, 2011; Dweck & Elliot, 1983; Shepard, 2000), performance goal structures have been associated with negative patterns of learning (Ryan, Gheen, & Midgely, 1998; Self-Brown & Mathews, 2003). As Kaplan, Gheen, and Midgley (2002) reported in their study on classroom goal structure and student behavior, "In mastery oriented classrooms, these practices emphasize to students that their main purpose in being in school is to learn, improve, and master the material, rather than to demonstrate high ability and conform to the teacher's goals" (p. 204). Furthermore, Dweck (2010) argues that the teacher's orientation toward supporting a learning environment as compared to a performance environment is a critical component of student success. Students take cues from teachers as to the extent that the purpose of their efforts in a classroom are to complete tasks quickly, prove one's ability, and accumulate points toward grades or to engage in challenging tasks and embrace errors as feedback as an opportunity to further one's learning (Pedersen & Williams, 2004; Romanowski, 2004).

A culture of learning and a culture of performance are analogous to an athletic team's practices as compared to their games. Practice is about learning; we focus on learning key strategies and attacking our weaknesses through a lot of discussion and repetition. If we make a mistake, we do the drill over again. If something is particularly difficult, we keep doing it. We acknowledge our weaknesses. We say as a team, "We can't do this yet, but wait until game day!" When game day comes, we are in a culture of performance. Everything counts. Mistakes count against us. We can't hit the restart button. For a team that is always immersed in a culture of performance, every day feels like a tryout or a game day. You'd go out of your way to avoid the areas of your game you need to improve most because you don't want to expose any liabilities. Unfortunately, when you ignore your weaknesses, you never have the chance to improve.

In the opening anecdote for this chapter, we described two very different classrooms. The first classroom appears to emphasize a performance environment; everything counts or counts against you. There is an emphasis on points and grades rather than learning. Furthermore, this classroom seems to emphasize answers over inquiry. Mathematics seems to be a process whereby the teacher shows the steps to follow, the teacher assigns problems, and then students find the right answer.

As we discussed in Chapter 3, too often learners believe that they are born with a fixed set of abilities that determine whether or not they are good at reading, or math, or art. From this lens, both success and failure are beyond one's control. Learners with high levels of self-efficacy are more likely to see success as affirmation of their effort and strategy. Furthermore, these learners do not see failure as affirmation of a lack of capacity but as a catalyst to focus efforts to develop new strategies. A school culture that values self-efficacy will be intentional in teaching students that patience, persistence, and strategy are more important than innate intelligence. A culture that supports cognitive engagement and builds passionate learners needs to find a balance between a culture of learning and a culture of performance. Students need a space that is safe for them to say they are learning, and it is acceptable to take risks and learn from mistakes.

Cognitive Engagement as a Culture of Inquiry or a Culture of Right Answers?

Have you ever gotten 20 pages into a novel and stopped reading? It might have been by a favorite author, well written, with good dialogue, but you stopped anyway. The reason we usually stop reading is simple; we've stopped asking questions. What propels us through a text are our questions: I wonder why . . . I wonder how that character will . . . I wonder what might happen next? But when those questions, your questions, stop, there is no need to continue reading.

What is of greater value in your classroom: asking a great question or giving the right answer? Of course there is content that students need to master. There are facts that educated people simply need to know. In a test-driven system of accountability, or on a trivia-based game show, knowing the right answer to decontextualized bits of information is always of value. But outside of multiple-choice tests and filling in the blanks on tax forms, putting the right answer in the blank is rarely valued as the critical skill that everyone must possess in today's society. In our mobile world, information is in your purse or your pocket. No longer is it of much value to be able to simply spout off the facts. As J. Russell and R. Cohn, authors of the article "Is Google Making us Stupid?" (2008) and Nicholas Carr, author of *The Shallows* (2010), argue, what matters most in this age is the ability to have deep enough understanding to formulate questions to sift through the noise and find the most valid, reliable, and useful information. Determining the best way to formulate a question is required before the process of seeking an answer can even begin.

We are born to ask questions. If you've ever spent time with a four-year-old, you've seen how strong this impulse is. Everything is a mystery. Everything requires an explanation. *Why is the sky blue? Why is the grass green? Why don't the cars all just smash into each other?* We are engaged in the world around us. We demand explanations. In our early years, these questions lead us to develop more understanding about how the world works than we will acquire in the rest of our lives. Unfortunately, early in our schooling process, we often shift away from this mode of inquiry to a passive mode of providing answers. Too often, students believe being smart means knowing all of the answers to other people's questions.

Typically, classroom culture requires students to wait passively and answer the teacher's questions. Students raise their hands when asked questions. Students take tests to answer questions. If we want to engage students cognitively, the questions need to flow in all directions. It is your questions that drive you to turn the next page of a novel; it is students' questions that drive them to be curious about what they might learn next. These are not your questions; these are the students' questions. A culture of inquiry honors the curiosity that others have about the world. They value the unknown and the unknowable. They understand that passionate learners do not prove their worth simply by providing someone else's answer to a question; they ask questions that haven't been asked before and are tenacious about uncovering answers.

Consider how these two classrooms might create very different norms, routines, and culture as related to the role of questions and answers in furthering understanding.

The first classroom has established a teacher-centered set of norms that support a culture of answers; the teacher is the hub for all communication and all interaction. Students are likely seated in rows with the teacher standing in front of the classroom. If you have a classroom discussion, the teacher will moderate who can talk and when. The teacher will ask all of the questions. Students raise their hands, tell the teacher their comments, and the teacher might tell him or her "No" or "Right" and move on to the next question. Early in the school year, a pattern takes hold; there are three or four students who always have their hands raised and always have the right answer. The other students merely watch. Or, perhaps the teacher uses questions to manage behavior; *if you are not paying attention, I will ask you a question that you will not know the answer to and you will be embarrassed in front of your peers!*

Now, consider the other classroom that supports a culture of inquiry. At the end of class, the teacher may give students an exit slip that reads:

- A question I have about today's lesson is: _____
- Based on what you learned today, if _____ were here right now (Pythagoras, Martin Luther King, Jr., Harper Lee, Cesar Chavez, Pablo Picasso, Albert Einstein, a Roman soldier . . .) what would you ask him or her?

The next day, two of those questions are on the board. Students come in and write about how they think the question should be answered. After writing, students pair share and generate new questions they are wondering about. A few of the students' questions are then posed to the class for a discussion.

In this inquiry-driven classroom, it may be completely normal for the teacher to sit in a circle along with the other students. In this classroom the culture allows for equal footing among all participants—including the teacher—during the discussion. No one raises a hand to await permission to speak. They make eye contact and speak with one another. The teacher waits his or her turn along with the other students. In this classroom, students may be more likely to ask questions of one another. The discussion may be more free-flowing. The discussion may wander off course—until another student helps the group refocus. The teacher is purposeful about using questions to further curiosity and understanding. The class is committed not to merely give the right answer but to struggle to understand the content and concepts more deeply and to ask the questions that will propel others to new levels of understanding.

The hallmark of a classroom that strives for cognitive engagement by building a culture of inquiry is this: In a classroom focused on right answers, the teacher's greatest fear is that a student might ask a question and he or she does not know how to answer. In a classroom focused on inquiry, the teacher believes that the lesson is not successful until students are asking questions that he or she does not know how to answer.

A CULTURE OF PURPOSE AND COMMITMENT TO SUPPORT EMOTIONAL ENGAGEMENT

A culture that supports passionate learners values high levels of emotional engagement. In these classrooms, students see one another as people, not just as other students. An emotionally engaged student does not simply show up to school in the morning and leave at the end of the day; he or she is interested in, and supported by, the people around him or her. Teachers care about him or her as a student and as a person. Classmates notice when he or she misses a day of school. He or she can ask questions in class without fear of being ridiculed. We believe a classroom culture that supports high levels of emotional engagement are committed to ensuring students strive to understand one another, rather than simply judge one another, and value the contributions and capacity of a classroom focused on we rather than just me.

To consider how important emotional engagement is to support a productive culture in classrooms and schools, consider this. Perhaps the greatest punishment children can bestow on another child is social isolation. A child can be called names for days—even weeks—and not tell another soul. But when a child is given the silent treatment, the frustration in that child's words and actions becomes so apparent so quickly that teachers almost immediately are attuned to the fact that there is a problem. Learning cannot occur when we are isolated from others. This makes sense when one thinks of a framework for human development like Maslow's (1943) hierarchy of needs. After basic physiological needs like food and shelter are met, we need to feel safe, and we need to belong. We need a purpose to survive, and that purpose is to be a part of something bigger than ourselves. As Mike Dickmann and Nancy Stanford-Blair (2009) argue, "Interaction with the brains of others . . . continues to be the primary means by which you exercise and refine your intellectual capacities" (p. 109). We cannot make meaning of our world and ourselves in isolation.

To be emotionally engaged means we are exhibiting positive feelings toward teachers, classmates, course work, and school. And emotional engagement begins with relationships. It is argued that "positive relationships with adults are perhaps the single most important ingredient in promoting positive student development" (Pianta, Hamre, & Allen, 2011, p. 370).

We know of a school that understood the importance of relationships. The staff decided to ensure that every student who did not seem to be well connected with other students had an informal mentor in their school. The teachers, custodians, paraprofessionals, support personnel, and principal each committed to developing a supportive relationship with one to three of these students. The process of establishing these connections began with every staff member making an effort to find these students and greet them on a daily basis, ask some questions about their interests, and learn about the individuals' talents and strengths. The adults were committed to making time to actively listen to these students and to be present when speaking with them. Not only did relationships improve for those at-risk students, but peer relationships became more positive and productive among all students. The school's climate transformed from one where many students felt connected and safe—but others were ostracized—to one where all students felt valued and supported.

Emotional Engagement as a Culture of Judging or a Culture of Understanding?

When your students see one another, do they look at each other like judges waiting to render a decision, or do they look each other like anthropologists trying to understand how others might see the world differently than they do?

We judge. We all do. We establish a set of beliefs about right and wrong and live our lives by these judgments. Most of the time, this is a good thing. Without these guideposts to anchor us, we wouldn't be able to tell people who we are, what we believe, or what we value.

Unfortunately, we can miss a lot of the good in each other when we use this habit of mind to make decisions about others. *People who are like me are good. People who are different than me are not good.* Adolescents can become particularly adept at this erroneous thinking. In a culture that supports each learner's need for emotional engagement, students need to be taught to see value in perspectives and values that are different from our own. In the 21st century, there is more value in diversity than ever before. Not only is there value in cultural diversity, but there is diversity of skill and thought.

For example, consider IDEO, the legendary design company that creates the look and feel of products for Apple and dozens of other cutting-edge companies. IDEO is a long way from the 1950s culture of men with identical education and backgrounds heading into their cubicles in matching grey flannel suits. The company intentionally hires individuals with diverse professional backgrounds to create teams that will take a novel approach to problem solving. There may be a designer and an engineer, but there also may be a biologist, a musician, a mathematician, and a historian. What is of value is their ability to work together, understand a problem, generate ideas, and render an elegant solution (Kelley & Littman, 2001).

For IDEO, richness of thought emerges from the synergy of the team. The team of the past might have consisted of a designer and a team of engineers. The designer served as the lone genius, and the engineers worked to tell the designer what was and was not possible. For the team of the past, the idea of putting a biologist or a historian on the team would have been met by judgment from the chosen few: *But what does a biologist know about beauty? What does a historian know about the tensile strength of molded plastic? He's not going to tell me anything. I will put her in her place.* But IDEO is successful because their teams strive to see the system as a whole. Their teams understand that the purpose can be understood only if the product is seen from the perspective of the user. Their teams understand that there is a commitment to working together to find the better idea. Their teams understand that these ways of thinking are not possible without the diversity of thought that is required to find elegant solutions to today's challenges.

Consider how these two classrooms might create very different norms, routines, and culture as related to the role of judging others or understanding one another as a pathway to deeper understanding.

The rules in the first classroom seem to communicate a message that it is your job to do your work—the right way the first time—and I am here to judge you. This could be manifest in how the teacher scores student work. Every day, students give their work to the teacher as they come in the classroom. The teacher quickly stamps the work so he or she knows it was completed for the start of class. Then, the teacher gives the assignments back to random students. He or she reads the answers, students mark each answer on the paper in front of them as right or wrong, and then the students place a score on top and pass the papers forward. Sometimes students make comments about others' scores, "Ohh, Demetrius got a 45!" Rather than confront that student, the teacher tells Demetrius to start studying and stop watching television.

This culture of judgment might also be apparent in how class proceeds after assignments are turned in. Each day after assignments are turned in, the teacher moves on to the next day's lesson. He or she demonstrates a few sample problems, gives the homework assignment, and gives students time to start their work. Talking—even if asking a classmate for help—is not tolerated. If you have a question about the work, the teacher often responds with something along the lines of "Pay attention next time. Read pages 245 to 247, and if you still can't do it, come up here and ask me." The assumption seems to be that if you don't get it, there is nothing anyone can do to help you. If you are not following the rules, it is due to a personal deficiency that you and you alone possess, and you'd better not let it get in the way of the others' learning. If you have a legitimate question, it should be done in private, so you don't bother the others' ability to finish their work.

The teacher in this classroom views compassion as a liability. Students pick up on his or her cues and are decidedly cynical toward one another. Absent the ability to work together and support each other, resentment builds within the classroom among students who struggle. Frustration mounts. Some students simply give up.

Now, consider the second classroom that builds emotional engagement by fostering a culture of understanding of one another.

In the second classroom, there is an intentional effort to create a supportive context for one another. Rather than framing the rules around a series of judgmental rewards and consequences, they are based on the support we can provide one another to ensure understanding. Furthermore, the rules are framed around the premise that only by understanding one another can we eliminate barriers to deep understanding of our content. In this classroom, the teacher starts each day greeting students at the door. He or she knows their names. The teacher knows their interests, needs, and strengths. "How was the game last night, Sonia? You had some great questions yesterday, Sam. I can't wait to see how you solved those equations! We'll need your best thinking today, Hannah. I'll need one of your metaphors to help others understand some new concepts."

Once students are in the classroom, they've established a two-minute routine whereby students can share good news. Sometimes a student may share a personal accomplishment, something positive that happened at home, or a word of thanks to a classmate who was helpful. Before starting this strategy, the teacher thought it would take up too much time. But the opposite turned out to be true. Students wanted to share quick anecdotes or hear a public word of thanks. It was as though the kids' words each day helped to let the tension out of the room. As kids were more compassionate with one another, the mood of the classroom grew more focused and relaxed. Kids needed fewer reminders to follow directions. They liked their teacher. The rules were fair. They learned a lot in the classroom, and they didn't want to disappoint the teacher.

As they delved into the content of class, students were comfortable asking questions. In fact, after a question that seemed to cause everyone to pause, the teacher would say, "Thumbs-up if you are wrestling with the same question." Depending on the result, the teacher would go back and spend more time on that skill or concept. Students knew they could ask without being judged. Students knew their questions were important. Before giving the assignment, the teacher would give a formative sample problem and have students solve the problem and then explain their answers in triads. If there is any confusion about concepts or steps, students need to frame clarifying questions that the other groups would attempt to answer.

Students in this classroom knew that there were no dumb questions. Students knew that the goal was to ensure everyone understands, and understanding only emerges through perseverance. In fact, any time a student was really struggling to understand something, the teacher could be heard saying "If you understood this already, I'd move you up to the next class. I used to get stuck on some of these same concepts before it finally clicked for me."

Emotional Engagement as a Culture of Me or We?

Do your students see school as an individual endeavor that is about *me* or as a set of opportunities that *we* must engage together in order to produce our best work? Typically, school is seen as an individual set of tasks that everyone engages in separately but at the same time. *We* are given the same assignments each night, and *I* do my work. *We* are given a book to read, and *I* do my reading.

We are given an essay, and *I* do my writing. The notion that we are all assigned the same task and we all go to our separate corners and do the same work is in stark contrast to the work we engage in the real world in two important ways.

First, jobs where everyone generates the same work are being automated or outsourced like never before (Friedman, 2005); only on an assembly line would everyone do the same task, in the same way, at the same time, in an attempt to yield an identical product. In 21st-century jobs that cannot be automated or outsourced, individuals are engaged in work that provides a unique contribution to a collective whole. If individuals do work on specific components of projects or products, they are a part of a larger collective whole that could not function without individuals working together.

Second, working in isolation prevents us from doing our best work. Two brains are better than one. A key contributor to learning is our ability to rely on others for feedback that clarifies and furthers our thinking. Openness to feedback is more likely to occur in a context where we trust those with whom we are working. When individuals are led to believe that the work they do is exclusively about them, they experience a rude awakening when working in an authentic context as a team. They need to listen. They need to be patient. They need to ask important, clarifying questions. They need to acknowledge the better idea. They need to provide emotional support when others are frustrated. This is the context in which students will be generative into the 21st century. Absent a commitment to a shared purpose, rather than a commitment to one's individual agenda, individuals will not have the skills required to transcend their own self-interests to better serve a team.

If most of what we learn is from working with others, and if our capacity to be generative is increased by working with others, why is so much of school such a solitary endeavor? In a classroom purely focused on me, a student can come and go as he or she pleases without even knowing the names of those around him or her, let alone trusting, interacting with, and learning from others. This is exacerbated when competition, rather than teamwork, is viewed as the catalyst that best supports learning. In a competitive environment that emphasizes grading on a curve or class rank, individuals become even more focused on the question: *What is in this for me?* In this environment, there is little or no incentive to support others' learning because a win for them is a loss for me. We know of a high school that eliminated class rank many years ago. The year after the new policy was put into place, the librarian (we said it was many years ago!) noticed that fewer books were missing, and fewer books were misplaced on the shelves. Her hypothesis was that there was less incentive for students to sabotage each other's learning.

Consider the two classrooms described in the beginning of this chapter. The first classroom emphasizes a culture of *me*, while the second emphasizes a culture of *we.*

In the first classroom, the rules are framed around a dichotomy of *me* and *them.* It is the lone wolf against the pack. The premise seems to be that students are pitted against one another. The premise seems to be that the teacher is pitted against the students. While tennis is something that is clearly important to the teacher, the character of the classroom seems to end there. In sharing an interest in tennis with students, the teacher makes him- or herself more human, which is to be commended. But make no mistake; this is the teacher's room, with the teacher's stuff, and the teacher's rules.

The me–we dichotomy also comes to play on days before and after tests. The class would play a game called Survivor, where students were given a series of problems to solve that grew incrementally more challenging. Students would solve the problem and write their answers on a small wipe board. If a student got the problem wrong, he or she was out. If the student got the problem right, he or she kept going. When it was down to the final three, the final problem was a race; the first person finished with the correct answer was given five extra-credit points on the test; the second-place finisher was given three extra-credit points, and the third-place finisher was given one extra-credit point on the test. Everyone knew which five students would be vying for the top three spots at the end of the game; they were always the same five students. Furthermore, they were the students who least needed any extra-credit points on their tests. Survivor created a competitive wedge among students; they would argue for one measly point.

In the second classroom, the language is predicated on what *we* will do to support one another's learning and why *we* are learning mathematics. Not only are the rules framed in positive terms, but the students helped with the language of the rules and signed off on them. There is a shared commitment to these rules—an awareness that the rules are in place not simply to be punitive but to support the collective goal of the group: to learn mathematics. As already articulated, the methods utilized in this classroom are based on a belief that knowledge is constructed through a process of building meaning.

A CULTURE OF PURPOSE TO SUPPORT BEHAVIORAL ENGAGEMENT

A culture that supports passionate learners values high levels of behavioral engagement. In these classrooms, students see value in the work that they do because they believe it is challenging, relevant, and meaningful. A behaviorally engaged student does not merely turn in work for points and grades; he or she is curious about learning and is eager to learn. We believe that cultures that support high levels of behavioral engagement are committed to establishing a culture of high rather than low expectations for all students. Additionally, these classrooms establish a purpose for learning that emphasizes intrinsic motivation and productivity rather than external manipulation and compliance.

Behavioral Engagement in a Culture of Compliance or Authenticity?

Do students do their work to avoid consequences or because they believe their work is relevant and meaningful? Do students persevere through challenging problems because they are committed to finding the best answer or because they merely want the points and grades?

Behavioral engagement is concerned with the extent that students are invested in actions that contribute to their learning. When students are authentically engaged, the values and strategies the school relies upon to support students' cognitive and emotional needs are aligned to the behaviors and tasks students are asked to utilize to accomplish their goals. A challenge with identifying students' levels of engagement is that students can play the game in a manner that makes them appear behaviorally engaged, while in reality, they are merely being compliant.

In the first chapter, we described some key distinctions between a cognitive-humanist approach to engagement and a behaviorist approach to compliance; the behaviorist system relies on extrinsic motivation, while the cognitivist-humanist relies on intrinsic motivation. We describe the significance of these distinctions in more detail as we use this dichotomy to better understand the role of the behavioral engagement that is so evident when working with passionate learners.

Authentic engagement (Schlechty, 2011) is characterized by students purposefully engaged in tasks or activities because those tasks or activities are of personal value and interest to them. In other words, the goals—and the process to attain those goals—are the same for both the student and the school. This could include a child who loves ceramics working on a ceramics project for an upcoming show or a student who is intrigued by physics trying to solve an equation that he or she believes will explain an interesting phenomenon. Or, this could mean that the goal of the course is to teach students to make inferences from complex texts. Rather than asking all students to read the same text, students may be given choices, so the content is aligned to their personal interests. When these components are aligned, the meaning and purpose of the task do not depend on external reward or manipulation. The rewards of being generative, solving meaningful problems, communicating important findings, and so on are intrinsically rewarding on their own terms.

The behaviorist view stands in stark contrast to the example of authentic engagement. Extrinsic, rather than intrinsic, rewards and punishments are seen as the primary means to shape behavior. Schools often adopt this behaviorist view by creating a token economy (Kohn, 1999) to motivate students. The assumption is that absent a token incentive to do the task (such as points and grades) or a tangible set of consequences (such as zeros or demerits) students will not do their work. This assumption is based on two anachronistic beliefs about teaching and learning: (1) students only learn when given a token reward, and (2) if students don't do work, it is because the token incentive is not large enough or the token punishment is not strong enough. Research on behaviorist-influenced, performance-oriented goal structures as compared to more cognitive-humanist, learning-oriented goal structures demonstrates that these behaviorist premises may not only be wrong, but they actually may undermine student motivation and student learning (Ames & Archer, 1988; Crooks, 1988; Dweck, 2000; Stiggins, 2001).

To the behaviorist, what the learner thinks about the rules or the task is less important than whether or not the rules are followed and the task gets done. *The goal is compliance.* If students are not doing their work or following the rules, the problem is likely deemed to be that the rewards aren't high enough or the consequences are not strong enough. So, if there is an issue in a school that too many students are arriving tardy to class, a behaviorist approach would establish a reward such as incentive field trips and exam exemptions for those who arrive on time and a consequence of more school, assessments, and perhaps some demerits and detentions for those who don't. Similarly, if students aren't doing their work, it is because the consequences are deemed to be too weak; if zeros won't motivate them to do their work, detentions will!

We believe there are three primary problems with the behaviorist approach to accepting compliance as a proxy for behavioral engagement.

First, behaviorist approaches can extinguish intrinsic motivation because the tangible rewards are deemed to be, and eventually accepted as, more important than intrinsic rewards (Pink, 2009). For example, a child who enjoys playing the piano for hours on end may find him- or herself playing less often when the teacher requires practice and keeps track of practice time each day. The child is no longer playing for enjoyment and stops playing the music he or she loved. Suddenly, the purpose of playing is to be in compliance with the practice log. When teachers frame school in terms of points and grades, should we be surprised that some kids will monitor every point in an attempt to get a high grade—whether they are learning or not? Conversely, for students who are struggling, they may acquiesce partway through the grading period by saying something along these lines: "The most amount of points I can get anyway is only worth a D, and that is if I get a hundred on the rest of my tests. Why bother even trying?"

Second, behaviorist approaches actually can encourage cheating. Sometimes tightening the screws on compliance can result in students thinking something that sounds something like this: "If my teacher doesn't really care if I understand it anyway, and all she ever talks about are points and grades, and I need at least a B+ to go out this weekend, what is the big deal?" The reality is that students who doubt their abilities and are concerned about their grades are more likely to cheat (Rafanelli, 2012). Even more cynically, a student who cheats simply may have given up on him- or herself and the system. A student who knows there will be consequences for saying "I tried but couldn't get my work done because I didn't get it, but my teacher can't explain it to me anyway" will find a way to beat the system because he or she believes it can't support his or her learning.

Third, we believe the greatest challenge to the behaviorist approach is that it often assumes that students have the skills to do their work; they simply choose not to. Similarly, it assumes students have the self-control to follow the rules; they simply choose not to. When this occurs, a legitimate opportunity to support a student's learning is missed because laziness or apathy is determined to be the culprit—and not the disconnect between the child's learning needs and the misalignment of opportunities that have been provided to the child. Ironically, this response may cause further alienation and disengagement from school (Glasser, 1998; Kohn, 2006; Pierson & Connell, 1992). When this occurs, a struggling learner has not only been punished because of a failure of the institution that was supposed to teach him or her, but the child is punished a second time with punitive consequences. This would be akin to a physician withholding medicine from a patient with heart disease for failing to stay on an exercise regimen.

These behaviorist approaches made sense in the industrial era of scientific management. As Daniel Pink (2009) explains, behaviorist systems of reward and punishment are efficient and effective when individuals are asked to engage in boring, repetitive tasks. If I am going to get you to produce 700 widgets a day, the work will grow tedious. If there is an added incentive to hit the 700 mark, and a consequence if you don't, that could motivate you to comply. However, make no mistake; few people would simply volunteer to make widgets all day. There is little or nothing cognitively engaging about the task. In a loud factory with few breaks, there is little opportunity to build emotional connections to engage with others. Therefore, to elicit behavioral compliance, rewards and incentives are the only remaining path.

But shouldn't schools be built around tasks and learning opportunities that are engaging on their own terms? In a culture of authenticity, students engage in work because it is purposeful; there are important problems to be solved. Skills aren't learned in a vacuum of *you will need this someday;* the purpose is to apply those skills to solve authentic problems that exist *today.* This culture of authenticity begins with a very different premise than a purely behaviorist culture. Rather than assuming people do their best work through rewards and threats, the authentic culture assumes that people want to do good work and are most likely to be passionate about their learning when taught the skills—and given the permission—to guide their own learning.

The best example of the intersection among cognitive and emotional engagement that results in extremely high levels of behavioral engagement that we know of is *flow.* Authenticity, passion, and commitment are central to this concept.

Flow is a state of mind whereby individuals are deeply immersed in thought and action that incorporates equal elements of work and play (Csikszentmihalyi, 1990). When in this state, individuals report being so deeply engaged that they lose sense of time and space. This flow experience includes several key components: (1) It is a challenging activity that requires skill; (2) it requires a balance between action and awareness, or metacognition; (3) there are clear goals and the opportunity for specific feedback; (4) the individual concentrates deeply on the task at hand; (5) there is a clear sense of personal control in the experience; (6) these components result in a loss of self-consciousness (not consciousness); and (7) a transformation of time. The flow experience is driven from within by intrinsic motivators. Mihaly Csikszentmihalyi explains that

> Flow lifts the course of life to a different level. Alienation gives way to involvement, enjoyment replaces boredom, helplessness turns into a feeling of control, and psychic energy works to reinforce the sense of self, instead of being lost in the service of external goals. When experience is intrinsically rewarding life is justified in the present, instead of being held hostage to a hypothetical future gain. (1990, p. 69)

Research on student engagement from the perspective of flow theory (Shernoff, Csikszentmihalyi, Scheider, & Shernoff 2003) further clarifies the conditions under which high school students report being engaged and experiencing flow. In their study on student engagement and flow theory in high school classrooms, Shernoff and colleagues conducted a longitudinal study of 526 high school students across the United States. To conduct this study, students wore pagers (remember them?), and when the pager went off, the students would write what they were doing in school at that exact moment and then rate their level of concentration, interest, and enjoyment. Students reported the highest levels of engagement when they perceived the challenge of the task and their own skills to be in alignment, the topic was relevant to their own lives, and they had some control over their learning environment. They reported that students spent an average of one-third of their time passively attending to information transmitted to the entire class and half of their time doing independent work. In fact, disengagement may be the result of a lack of challenge or meaning reported by students as occurring in the typical lecture format. Overall, the researchers found that

> activities that are academically intense and foster positive emotions stand the best chance of engaging students. Ideally, teachers may develop activities that are experienced as challenging and relevant, yet also allow students to feel in control of their learning environment and confidence in their ability. Teachers succeeding in providing such engagement most likely consider not only the knowledge and skills to be learned, but also the students as learners, adapting instruction to their developmental levels and individual interests. (Shernoff et al., 2003, p. 173)

Csikszentmihalyi's work is extremely comprehensive in that his findings are rooted in historical research and have been replicated in numerous studies conducted around the world. His research transcends disciplines as it cited in psychology, education, sociology, and business. As a hallmark of behavioral engagement, the concept of flow should become a central point of understanding for educators committed to creating passionate learners.

Consider the two classrooms described in the beginning of this chapter. The first classroom emphasizes a culture of *compliance*, while the second emphasizes a culture of *authentic engagement*.

The rules of the first classroom clearly emphasize a system of rewards and consequences as the central means to gain compliance. When the teacher gives the assignment or is giving a lecture, he or she constantly tells students that "this will be important because it is worth 15 homework points," or "this will be important because it is on the test." He or she rarely makes connections to the ways mathematics can be used in the real world.

The homework on the whiteboard in the front of the room is arranged in two columns:

Assignment	Points
P. 223 1–31 odds	15

In discussing assignments with students, pages and points are always the focus of the conversation. Someone listening in might not even know they were talking about mathematics.

In fact, the crux of the entire class seems to be that if you don't follow the rules, you will be docked points. One can imagine a student who is having a hard time learning a new concept on the day's assignment who turns to a classmate for help. The student is called for a "fault" by the teacher. After being told sternly by the teacher, "Just because you don't get it doesn't mean Harper shouldn't be able to get her work done," the student has little interest in going to the teacher to ask for help. That night, the student struggles with his or her assignment and, despite working on it for almost a couple of hours, fails to complete problems 29 and 31. The next day, when the teacher realizes the work is incomplete, the student is reprimanded. "Yesterday you were bothering others, and today your work isn't completed. That's a minus five for you." The student begins to counter the teacher's interpretation of the rules, but the teacher merely points to the rule sheet. The student, frustrated, decides the argument is not worth his or her time.

At no point is the conversation between the teacher and the student about the mathematical skills or concepts central to the reason for doing the work. Supporting one another to use more effective strategies is never discussed. In this culture of compliance, following the rules and accepting the consequences seem to be the purpose of the course.

In the second classroom, a decidedly different scenario unfolds, a scenario that emphasizes authentic reasons for doing the work.

Students can select among a pool of problems to solve. As a part of the assignment, students write real-world story problems that (1) are relevant to something of interest to them and (2) utilize the concepts and skills in the day's assignment. Students make connections that would have never crossed their minds; from volleyball to stock car racing or gas prices, students find connections to their interests. As we explained earlier as related to cognitive engagement in the second classroom, students are expected to actively discuss their understandings and questions before leaving the classroom. Students not only see the work as relevant, but they engage their classmates as resources that help them see the relevance and meaning of their work. The assignments are written on the whiteboard in two columns as well, but they are framed this way:

| the terms of the assignment are _____ | to build your understanding of _____ |

The first component articulates the task; the second component articulates the learning goal—the authentic reason the skill is of value in the real world.

When the teacher in the second classroom explains the importance of the work, it is rarely in terms of points or grades; it is almost always in terms of helping students accomplish the short-term goals they've established for their own learning, or it is communicated in terms of real-world application. Students do their work without much badgering. When they don't do their work, he or she pulls them aside and asks if something personal is interfering with their ability to do their work. Because they trust the teacher, they tell him or her. If it is an issue of understanding, they don't talk about points and grades, rather they talk about mathematics. They talk about the strategies they are using to complete these types of problems. If they are not working, they look at the front wall and find another strategy that might work even better. "I know you can do this. We just haven't found the best strategy yet."

Behavioral Engagement as a Culture of Low Expectations or Expertise?

Do your students do their work just to get it done or because they believe they are on a path toward mastery and expertise?

Finishing a task and becoming expert are two very different things. Anders Ericsson is the world's foremost expert on expertise. He has researched and written extensively about how experts engage their work in very different ways than individuals who plateau early and fail to reach their true capacity. As we discussed in Chapter 3, this plateau is often attributed to a fixed mindset about intelligence. Most people assume that they've reached their genetic limit to their capacity and accept those limits by simply acquiescing; they lower their standards and accept their plateau as their maximum level of performance. The fixed mindset becomes a self-fulfilling prophecy.

Ericsson and his colleagues believe that few people ever approach the true limits of their capacity. In fact, they argue that there is little empirical evidence that innate ability is the limiting factor in one's ultimate performance; anyone can make dramatic improvements in their performance well beyond the initial performance plateau (Ericsson & Charness, 1994). Experts are unique from other practitioners in a domain because they've developed a varied and replicable skill set that allows them to utilize the right strategy, in the right way, to obtain the specific results they desire.

While students cannot become experts in mathematics, or writing, or history, or craftsmanship within their K–12 experience, the pathway toward expertise and the productive habits of mind that are internalized by experts can be valued by educators and taught to students. This will allow them both to adopt a set of skills and behaviors that support their efforts to make dramatic improvements in any area they choose. Specifically, Ericsson, Prietula, and Cokely (2007) argue that experts utilize the following strategies and dispositions to improve.

Experts practice deliberately—Experts are tenacious about finding specific areas of need and engaging in deliberate practice. Deliberate practice means identifying a specific aspect of a performance and practicing it over and over. Most people who plateau gravitate toward practicing areas where they are already good. Think of the young piano player who gets really good at a certain song and then starts to play only that one song or the student who really enjoys reading nonfiction and never practices a different set of comprehension strategies required to read fiction. The concert violinist practices a challenging passage again and again.

The aspiring Olympic figure skater will fall again, and again, and again, practicing the most challenging jumps that others don't even dare to try. The mathematician wrestles with the problem that can't be solved again and again—trying slightly different strategies each time.

Experts take their time—Expertise does not emerge overnight. Expertise takes time. Ericsson argues that it takes about 10,000 hours of deliberate practice to obtain expertise in a specific domain. That is roughly 10 years of practice for 20 hours each week. This does not mean merely doing something for that period of time; it means being strategic about identifying specific weaknesses and specific areas of need and confronting those weaknesses by learning new strategies, or honing existing strategies, to improve.

Experts respond to feedback—As we discussed in Chapter 4, feedback is among the key accelerators or inhibitors of learning. Quality, formative feedback allows learners to modify and improve their performance by focusing their efforts on key areas to improve. Experts have a voracious appetite for feedback. They desperately want to know what is working and what is not working, so they can continue to hone their understanding or their technique.

Experts observe others and work closely with coaches—Experts do not work in isolation. They are students of their disciplines. They watch others engage in their crafts to see how they deploy skills and strategies in ways that help them be successful. They talk to others to learn about their areas of strength and how they improved. They talk to others to learn about their frustrations in their efforts to improve and better understand that the pathway toward expertise is littered with failed attempts that were turned into opportunities to learn.

There are many great ways to help students understand these four pathways toward expertise. For example, the best athletes and actors in the world all have coaches. They work on the weakest portions of their performance, they seek and listen to feedback, and they closely watch the performances of the individuals they aspire to emulate.

In stark contrast to a classroom that supports a culture of mastery and the habits of mind of those who aspire to become experts is a classroom that has established a culture of low expectations. There are two components to a culture of low expectations: the expectations students hold of themselves to produce high-quality work and the expectations of adults to hold students accountable to produce work that is of high quality.

First, students in a culture of low expectations typically operate from one of two sets of assumptions. The first set is associated with students who believe they are not capable of producing high-quality work. Perhaps they have fixed mindsets about learning, or perhaps they've spent years in school simply treading water, not really understanding but getting grades that are good enough to get them by. These students have low expectations of what they are capable of as learners. Rather than investing time in efforts that are unlikely to result in understanding, they make conscious decisions to invest little time, effort, or energy into their work. Good enough means just good enough to pass or good enough to avoid consequences at home.

The second set of assumptions observed in a culture of low expectations is associated with students who believe they are capable of producing high-quality work but don't think their teacher notices (or cares). For example, these students may invest a significant amount of time and energy in doing a project that is of high quality and find they obtain the exact same feedback and grades as their classmates. These students adjust their level of expectations for quality to the lowered expectations of the teacher. These students determine the minimal amount of work they need to do in order to obtain a high grade and invest their efforts accordingly.

The second component of a culture of low expectations is driven by the assumptions of the adults who control the learning environment. When adults have low expectations for learners, they typically do one of three things: They fail to ask students to be purposively generative, they ask students to produce work that may be of little intellectual rigor, and they fail to hold students accountable for quality work.

Low expectations as a failure to ask students to be purposively generative—In a culture of low expectations, teachers may minimize the amount of work students are asked to produce. This can emerge from good intentions. The teacher does not want students to struggle or get frustrated. The teacher does not want to ask any questions of a student during class time because he or doesn't want to embarrass the student. But if the work is too challenging, the teacher needs to step back and consider the strategies that might make the work manageable. How can the task be broken into smaller pieces? What scaffolds can be utilized that help the student build from manageable to more sophisticated work? What components of the task can the student do well to use as a catalyst to move forward with more challenging work? The purpose in purposively generative, high expectations doesn't mean we ask kids to simply produce a lot of work. Churning out worksheets or doing hundreds of identical mathematics problems is not indicators of high expectations.

*Low expectations as a failure to ask students to do work that lacks rigor—*Rigor is not merely a function of quantity. Students can be asked to write a 20-page paper or complete 500 multiple-choice problems, but neither of these scenarios provides any indication about the level of rigor required of students to be successful. Whether using a scale like Bloom's taxonomy (1956) or Webb's Depth of Knowledge scale (1997), rigor is about the level of depth and sophistication required of a learner to complete a task successfully. It is much easier to teach and grade a factual statement about Abraham Lincoln than it is to teach and assess a student's development and utilization of criteria to evaluate Lincoln's effectiveness on domestic policy as compared to other presidents. To ask students rigorous questions means we are committed to helping students persevere through the ambiguity of questions that do not have easy answers. Perhaps the greatest challenge we create for ourselves when we fail to ask students to do rigorous work is that not only do we end up with curriculum and assessments that are decontextualized and disconnected from complexity of the real world, but we give students the false impression that they understand. There is little value in answering 100 multiple-choice questions that ask students to identify the correct definition of 100 vocabulary words. Even worse, a student who answers all those items correctly might earn an A on the test but fail to be able to apply the concepts that underlie those words to any type of meaningful, complex problem.

*Low expectations as a failure to hold students accountable for high-quality work—*Some teachers may transcend the first two components of adult behaviors that contribute to a culture of low expectations and then fall short on the final component: holding students accountable for high-quality work. In this scenario, the work is purposeful, and the work is rigorous, but the work—regardless of its quality or sophistication—is simply deemed to be "excellent" or "awesome." Conversely, students may be told that something is incorrect, but there is no expectation for the students to follow up on the work and revise their errors. We are not saying that everyone cannot get an A. We are saying that we need to be unwavering in our commitment to articulating what quality work looks like. Furthermore, we need to give students accurate feedback to balance the challenge and support we will provide to move their work toward even higher levels of quality.

Regardless of one's personal philosophy toward teaching and learning, there is consensus that low expectations are detrimental to student learning. At the 91st annual meeting of the NAACP (Bush, 2000), an aspiring presidential candidate named George W. Bush gave a speech about his vision for education policy in the United States. In this speech, he decried the "soft bigotry of low expectations." In September of 2009, President Barack Obama (2009) gave a back-to-school speech in Arlington, Virginia. In his speech, he asked students to "set your own goals for your education—and to do everything you can to meet them. . . . The truth is, being successful is hard." When George W. Bush and Barack Obama agree on something, we should probably pay attention.

Consider the two classrooms described in the beginning of this chapter. The first classroom has established a culture of *low expectations,* while the second emphasizes a culture of *mastery toward expertise.*

In the first classroom, assignments and assessments always are graded immediately. The assignments and assessments always have a single right answer. Scoring one another's assignments is easy because the teacher states the correct answer for each item when doing the homework check. Tests are always multiple choice; you solve a problem and select from five options; the fifth is always none of the above. There is no mention of mathematical reasoning on these tests, nor is there any mention of mathematical reasoning in the classroom. You are given a problem, and you give an answer; it is either right or wrong.

Sometimes, when a student gets stuck on a problem and asks for help, the teacher replies with a genuine, "That one is tough. You don't need to worry about that one." A few weeks into the advanced classes, the teacher brings a few students together and quietly tells them that he or she is really concerned about their ability to do well in this class because it is so difficult and encourages them to drop it. They do so. His personal philosophy is that no student should be in an advanced class unless he or she has the natural ability to get an easy A.

In the second classroom, there is a decidedly different culture of expectations.

In this classroom, from day one, the teacher tells students that the reason the course is worth taking is because it is challenging. Furthermore, he or she tells them that the teacher's job is to support everyone's efforts not just to get an A, but to understand the material in a way that they can use to influence their world. Students engage in a goal-setting process that they monitor throughout the year. "Everyone is in a different place. We will all take a different path, but we will all get to the destination. My job is to help you find the path that will get you there" is another one of the mantras repeated frequently by the teacher in this classroom.

When new concepts are introduced in this classroom, the teacher really helps students break the skills and subskills of the problem down to smaller components, so students learn to diagnose where their strengths and weaknesses are. Once students become aware of an area of need, they identify specific problem sets that they will do in order to practice that skill repeatedly.

Students are asked to explain their thinking on every assignment. Explain the strategy you used and why. What other strategies might you have used? If the problem had been multiplication rather than addition, how would you have solved it differently? There are mathematical reasoning rubrics that the teacher uses to guide students' understanding of what it means to provide a *novel solution* or a *sophisticated explanation,* and by the end of the school year, students who didn't understand that those terms had anything to do with mathematics can now apply those rubrics to accurately assess and provide feedback to other students.

In previous chapters, we discussed the main pillars for creating passionate learners to involve mindset, internal dialogue, and self-determination. Each of these pillars has a distinct place in building a strong classroom culture. The teacher models the language expected of the classroom. The way the teacher speaks and asks questions influences the way students perceive themselves and the world around them. This language impacts how the students in and out of the classroom learn how to interact and learn from one another. When teachers and other staff in a building genuinely care about students and connect with them about

Table 6.1   Culture Non-Examples and Examples

Realm of Engagement	Non-Example	Example	Culture's internal condition of purpose and commitment is met by . . .
Emotional	• Culture of judgment • Culture of me	• Culture of understanding • Culture of we	. . . a classroom of cooperation. . . . setting goals and giving and using stakeholders feedback. . . . celebrating growth in learning. . . . students engaged in work so strongly that they are committed to the learning tasks.
Behavioral	• Culture of compliance • Culture of low expectations	• Culture of authenticity • Culture of high expectations	
Cognitive	• Culture of performance • Culture of answers	• Culture of learning • Culture of inquiry	

schoolwork, sports, or outside activities, students are more likely to invest effort in their schooling experience.

In Chapter 5, we spoke about the importance of self-determination. Self-determination is equally important in creating a culture of engagement. Teachers who give students a voice in giving feedback to the teacher about what is working or not working for their learning or give meaningful choice within an activity increase students' motivation (Pianta, Hamre, & Allen, 2011). Some teachers build voice directly into their classroom cultures. For example, a teacher may share the results of a formative assessment with a group of students and ask for feedback about what he or she can do in order to help the students learn the material. When the teacher actively listens and applies what the students have shared, the students are more likely to be motivated because they generate ideas to assist them in their learning. Phillip Schlechty (2011) says that to earn students' attention, a teacher needs to take the time to discover what motivates them.

Establishing a clear purpose for learning and a commitment to support one another's learning are central to a culture that supports passionate learners. When this occurs, the student and teacher transcend their individual interests and work together in a climate that emphasizes who we are. *We are* a group that accepts, trusts, challenges, and supports one another's learning.

Table 6.2   Toolbox to Create a Culture of Trust and Acceptance

Toolbox Ideas	Why the Idea Helps to Create a Culture of Trust and Acceptance
Defining and reflecting on the expectations for the school community, classroom, and classmates	It allows for the students and the teacher to share what each values, resulting in building community.
Students using the strategy of Five Whys in order to create a class mission statement	Using the technique of the Five Whys (in essence asking a question and asking why that particular statement is important each time) gives students the opportunity to share what is important in their lives. The mission statement can be shared as a daily ritual, bringing students together.
Creating a set of ground rules	The stakeholders create ground rules, which create a sense of ownership and highlight the importance of working as a team.
Interviewing classmates for connectedness	Students practice deep listening as they learn about a classmate. Students learn about having choice when deciding on how to present the information to the class. The interview allows students to get to know each other, which helps with acceptance.
Using continuous quality improvement (CQI) tools to improve processes in the classroom or discuss issues emerging.	The tools allow both students and teacher to be a part of the process, which opens up communication and promotes thoughtful decisions and insightful discussions.

Resources for CQI Tools: David Langford: http://www.langfordlearning.com/resources/; Future Force: Kids That Want to, Can, and Do! A Teacher's Handbook for Using TQM in the Classroom by Elaine McClanahan and Carolyn Wicks; and Jim Shipley and Associates: http://www.jimshipley.net

The toolbox ideas help the teacher and the students in the classroom create a culture of purpose and commitment. When students see the purpose of their work as relevant and meaningful and are committed to the challenge, ambiguity, and intrinsic rewards of learning challenging content and developing new skills, they are more likely to be emotionally, behaviorally, and cognitively engaged. When this occurs under the guidance of a teacher who can create a culture that ensures an appropriate balance of challenge and support, students are more likely to be passionate about their learning.

PASSION DEFLATORS

Making learning relevant so that students are committed to their own learning has positive results. Unfortunately, some learners' realities include conditions and actions that deflate their passion for learning. Teachers need to be aware of passion deflators, principals need to look for and root out the passion deflators, and the organization itself must make these anachronisms of pedagogy unacceptable. We've described some of these deflators in this chapter:

> In a culture that solely focuses on performance, cognitive engagement is deflated in a culture when . . .
>
>> The emphasis is placed on tasks or grades, rather than learning, as the purpose for school.
>>
>> Mistakes are not seen as learning opportunities but as something to be avoided at all costs.
>
> In a culture that solely focuses on right answers, cognitive engagement is deflated in a culture when . . .
>
>> The teacher's questions are always more important than the students' questions.
>>
>> Giving the right answer is always more important than asking the next question.
>>
>> Questions are seen as a sign of ignorance rather than inquisitiveness.

In a culture that focuses on judging others rather than understanding them, emotional engagement is deflated in a culture when . . .

Students don't think it is safe to be themselves.

Diversity of the group is seen as a liability rather than as a strength.

We assume ill intent in others' words and actions before we've attempted to understand them.

In a culture that focuses solely on individual needs of I or me rather than on accessing the strengths of the group, emotional engagement is deflated in a culture when . . .

Students compete, rather than cooperate, with one another.

Students are threatened by those with skills that they themselves do not possess.

Sabotage or personal attacks may be seen as acceptable ways to gain standing in the group.

In a culture that emphasizes compliance as a proxy for authenticity, behavioral engagement is deflated when . . .

Learning goals and tasks do not seem purposeful.

Following the rules is deemed to be more important than being interested in what one is learning.

Students see following the rules as the purpose of schooling.

The teacher yields power over students by calling them on technicalities; this may even occur publicly in a manner that humiliates as student.

In a culture that emphasizes low expectations, behavioral engagement is deflated when . . .

The learning lacks relevance and seems to be devoid of purpose or commitment to understanding.

What is easy to grade becomes a criterion for assignments rather than what is important and challenging to learn.

An imbalance of challenge and support by the teacher causes students self-doubt in their abilities as learners.

There is a lack of meaningful, developmental feedback, and students are rarely asked to respond to that feedback.

Students believe the teacher will evaluate all work in a similar way, regardless of dramatically different levels of quality.

REFLECTION—THE POWER TO CHANGE THE PASSION DEFLATORS

Understand, address, and change passion deflators by asking:

How do you assess and access students' prior knowledge before introducing new information?

What do you know personally about each student?

What type of instruction engages individual learners? How does your instruction strategy empower students?

Do students have input and choice in their learning?

Does your instruction fit your learning style or students' learning styles?

Do you help students see the relevance of what they are learning to their lives?

What strategies do you use to get students to take responsibility for their learning?

Is your classroom culture focused on learning or achievement?

Do you help students reflect on effort and its relationship to learning?

Do you communicate high expectations? Do those expectations reflect a growth mindset?

Have you established a climate of caring? Do students help one another when one is experiencing social or emotional challenges?

Do you give students specific, meaningful, and timely feedback?

As you learn from your students, how does it influence your next instruction?

THE TEACHER WHISPERER

Teachers are responsible for fostering each individual's learning. If the goal is to help students grow as learners, teachers should consider the following to create a culture of learning:

- Understand a student's interests and preferences to reach their inner motivations.
- See each student's gifts and strengths.
- Build trust from the first day of interaction.
- Develop community by learning about each individual.
- Help students understand that their community of learners is a great asset.

A key to building an environment of trust and respect begins with how the teacher uses language and structures the classroom environment. Autonomy in the learning process is crucial in creating students who learn to solve problems. For example, if procedures are built so that students enter the classroom and know that a question will be posted to delve deeper into a concept learned from the previous day, a culture of learning is created. The culture is one where students are independent, cooperative individuals who share and build upon one another's knowledge.

A teacher whisperer engages students by meeting their social, emotional, and academic needs, instills a growth mindset, understands how to inspire students to find their passions, and empowers students to explore ideas so that learning is inherent. Teacher whisperers are mindful of how they set up the classroom as well as how they address their students as individuals and as a group. For example, when a student doesn't have a pencil, the teacher doesn't publicly reprimand the student for not being ready to begin class. Instead, the teacher has a container of community pencils available so that students can continue working without being humiliated or interrupting their learning.

TEACHING TIP

Connecting to students' lives builds necessary relationships. Take two minutes a day for 10 days to connect with a student, so the student will feel that he or she matters as an individual and learner. Donald Graves (2006) says a teacher needs to know at least 10 things about a student in order to teach him or her.

Figure 6.3   Example of Engaging Learners and Passion Deflators

Engaging Learners	Passion Deflators
Josie walks into her classroom and signs in on the computer for attendance, lunch, and milk count. She gets her materials out on her desk, so she is ready for math, and then walks to the back carpet where other students are gathered in small groups. She joins a group of three already discussing the science concepts. Josie reads the reflection questions posted on the board and joins in on the conversation. The teacher joins the students at the back carpet and hears from representatives about their conversations to gauge the day's lesson. Next, the students create a community circle where they pair and share about that day's intended learning. The student leader asks one student to share. The student does and calls on another student to share. After five students have shared, the student leader of the day leads the group in the Pledge of Allegiance and student mission statement. The teacher briefly shares the daily objectives, and students walk to their desks to begin their lesson. The teacher opens the lesson by drawing students' attention to the math goal posted on the board . . .	Josie walks into class and sits down at her desk to wait for the teacher to begin the day. The teacher walks into the room and talks to two students who are not at their desks. The teacher takes attendance by calling each student's name. The students say, "Here" and tells the teacher whether they are having hot lunch and milk. The teacher asks the students to stand to recite the Pledge of Allegiance. The students sit down after the pledge, the teacher instructs them to take out their math books, and the teacher begins lecturing on the math concepts of the day.

Teachers must create trust in order to help students realize the efforts they put forth lead to future successes. Dweck (2000) states that when teachers stress effort, students are more apt to take risks. With increased expectations for students to be able to think critically and solve problems, it is increasingly important for students to feel free to try challenging and new experiences. Students will take risks when the teacher develops a culture where mistakes are celebrated as a part of learning. Teachers can develop this culture by sharing their own beliefs. One way to do this is through the language they use in the classroom. Dweck (2012) shares as examples these statements: "You did that quickly and easily. I'm sorry I wasted your time," and "Who had a terrific struggle? What did you do when you struggled?" (Dweck, personal communication). This type of phrasing clearly sends the message that this classroom is focused on learning, and struggling with challenges is celebrated. Figure 6.4 gives examples of questions that promote and take away from students' growth mindsets.

Another key piece to culture is creating conversations between the teacher and the student. In order to aid the reader, the authors have created a learner profile that highlights the Engagement Literacy Model of mindset, internal dialogue, self-determination, and culture. The learner profile will include time for the student to self-reflect, time for the teacher and student to communicate, and time for the teacher to give specific suggestions or feedback to the student.

CULTURE DISPOSITIONS

It is every parent's wish to have a teacher create a compassionate, collaborative culture in which students care for each other as a loving family would, to have classmates who accept students for who they are so that each student feels free to take risks.

Culture begins with the teacher and his or her mindset. For example, while interviewing candidates for a teaching position,

Figure 6.4   Actions and Words to Encourage or Discourage Risk Taking

Dos	Don'ts
What did you learn by trying that strategy?	I'm surprised that you chose that strategy.
Are there any celebrations of learning for someone who struggled today?	Some of you did a nice job today, but it is apparent that several of you need to practice more.
What are some other ways to think about this concept?	I showed you how to do the work. Just do it the way I demonstrated.
What progress have you made toward your goal?	Why haven't you accomplished your goal?

Figure 6.5 Learner Profile

Concepts of Engagement Literacy	Constructs for Interaction Between Teachers and Students	Guiding Questions	Initial and Doable Actions	Feedback Plan Priorities
Mindset	Motivation	What opportunities can you take to explore, learn, or take on new challenges?		
	Mastery	Why is it important to get lost in learning and persist with a task?		
Internal Dialogue	Efficacy	What messages do you say to yourself when taking on a new or challenging task that results in believing that you can do this?		
	Feedback	How do you use the feedback given to you? How do you prepare to give feedback?		
Self-Determination	Ownership	Why does it feel good when you are empowered in your own learning?		
	Autonomy	What decisions can you influence that cause you to be motivated?		
Culture	Purpose	What is your goal in _____?		
	Commitment	How do you show commitment?		

141

six excellent candidates were interviewed, each with diverse and exceptional backgrounds. While interviewing the last candidate of the day, the room became alive as a result of this candidate's energy, intellect, and compassion.

There was one defining moment when the interview team knew they had the right candidate. It came when the candidate had to share what they would do if faced with a scenario where they would be entering a classroom that had been riddled with dysfunction and lack of respect. The candidate, without batting an eyelash, said, "I would reset the culture of the classroom around individual student motivation." The candidate knew students, learning, and dispositions at their core. The response encompassed everything about the graphic on creating passionate learners as the candidate continued to speak to classroom culture, changing a student's internal dialogue, and creating a want for both self-determination and growth mindset. The interview team wanted their own children in that classroom.

A teacher who has an understanding of the importance of culture also understands the dispositions students need to be taught and the practices needed to enhance the culture of the classroom. Figure 6.6 explains how this works.

The dispositions in culture focus on purpose and commitment. Within purpose, the dispositions of communication, problem solving, application, and compassion are inherent. Students use these dispositions to work as a team to meet goals. Under commitment, the dispositions of influencing, awareness, tenacity, and perseverance are the guiding forces that builds a culture of trust, risk taking, and respect.

Possible Dark Sides to Dispositions

It is here that the authors would like to caution the reader that a good idea can cause more harm than good if implemented poorly. Helping students become self-aware about their dispositions and how to strengthen them is important. As the adults, we need to be mindful in how we share this information. Read the "Caution" box to find a list of cautions along with why they could potentially hurt students. Figure 6.7 (page 146) is a student self-reflection tool for thinking about culture.

Figure 6.6 Culture Through the Teacher's Eyes

Skills and dispositions to support key components of purpose **"We are contributing to things greater than ourselves through our purpose"**	Culture begins with strong relationships and an environment of trust and acceptance.		
	Skills/Dispositions	**Defined as**	**Supported by teachers who . . .**
	Communication "We are open to other's ideas"	Conveying and sharing ideas, thoughts, and feelings in a respectful manner and "avoiding overgeneralizations, distortions, and deletions" (Costa & Kallick, 2014, p. 23)	. . . ask open-ended questions and teach students to learn more from a speaker by asking, "Tell me more about . . . " . . . teach students to ask questions to understand the ideas of others. . . . listen deeply and teach students to do the same with one another. One exercise might be for students to take turns being a speaker, listener, and observer (Costa & Garmston, 2002).
	Problem Solving "We are doing important work, and we are going to find a way to figure this out" Students who think aloud while solving problems approach problems more carefully and reason with greater accuracy (Whimbey, 1980).	The ability to use skills, strategies, and resources to find a solution that is correct or a solution that is more sophisticated, creative, insightful, thoughtful, accurate, or efficient	. . . strive for a balance of challenge and support (Saphier, Haley-Speca, & Gower, 2008). . . . help students understand that knowing an answer at a surface level and solving a problem that requires deep understanding require different skills and strategies (Hattie, 2012). . . . be aware of the level of rigor of various assessment tasks, and align strategy instruction and scaffolding to help students develop the skills to solve problems that are complex, open-ended, and may have more than one right answer (Bloom, 1956; Webb, 1997). Have students develop authentic problems with real-world connections and applications (Prast & Viegut, 2015).

(Continued)

Figure 6.6 (Continued)

	Defined as	Supported by teachers who ...
Application "We are going to apply what we've learned"	Solve problems by applying acquired knowledge, facts, techniques, and rules in a different way (Bloom, 1956)	... give students opportunities to apply new knowledge to real-life problems (Bloom, 1956). ... build curriculum around important concepts that kids can connect with content and questions that are important to them (Berns & Erickson, 2001).
Compassionate "We are able to empathize and see from the perspectives of others"	To understand how another person feels, which motivates the person to want to help (Costa & Kallick, 2008)	... model compassion in showing concern for students beyond academics. ... share stories from their lives that illustrate compassion. ... use books or historical or current people to point out instances of compassion. ... find a way to incorporate a service-learning project into your curriculum (Prast & Viegut, 2015).
Skills/Dispositions	**Defined as**	**Supported by teachers who ...**
Skills and dispositions to support key components of commitment **"We are dedicated to our learning and showing it through our commitment"** Influencing "We are interested in contributing to causes greater than ourselves"	Understanding how to work with others for a preferred future; key skills include building trust, seeing the strengths in others, following words with action, presenting ideas, making compromises, encouraging and connecting with others, and asserting self	... build a community of trust (Bryk & Schneider, 2002). ... ask students to share during a morning meeting or homeroom good news, a positive anecdote, or a thank-you to their classmates. ... demonstrate and model your commitment to learning and the importance of persevering despite difficulties and being tenacious in accomplishing a goal (Dweck, 2000; Ericsson & Charness, 1994). ... establish a commitment to one another's learning; put it on paper, and sign it.

Aware "We are attuned to others"	The ability to sense one's own and others' feelings and perceptions	. . . use books to talk about how the characters are feeling and what evidence from the book allows students to know that to be true. . . . demonstrate with-it-ness in the classroom by being aware of management issues and students' needs for engagement (Marzano, 2007). . . . model awareness by verbally sharing the ability to perceive how another is feeling and showing empathy.
Tenacious "We are going to figure this out—no matter what"	A stick-with-it mentality, being able to forego other opportunities in order to accomplish a goal over time (Dweck, Walton, Cohen, 2011).	. . . allow students a chance each day to begin again. . . . help students develop a growth mindset; the mind is like a muscle, and with exercise it gets stronger (Dweck, Walton, & Cohen, 2011).
Perseverance "We are going to utilize different strategies until we get this done well"	Persisting on a task until it is complete even when faced with challenges (Costa & Kallick, 2008)	. . . focus on intrinsic motivation and persevering through meaningful problems as their own reward (Wielsen, 2014). ˙ . . . teach students the components of deliberate practice (Ericsson, Prietula, & Cokely, 2007). . . . model and encourage an internal locus of control (Rotter, Chance, & Phares, 1972). . . . use stories of people (historical, current, fictional, or his or her own) who failed but continued trying.

Figure 6.7 Internal Conditions of Purpose and Commitment That Support Passionate Learners

	Indifferent	Compliant	Engaged	Passionate
Communication	We are aggressive, negative, and sometimes annoying when communicating as a group.	We are communicating in ways that keep us out of trouble.	We are sharing ideas, thoughts, and feelings in a respectful way.	We are contributing to things greater than ourselves through our purpose. We approach learning through our abilities to communicate, problem solve, apply, and show compassion. We routinely employ a framework such as plan, do, study, and act into our work.
Problem Solving	We are giving up without truly trying to solve the problem.	We are working on problems to finish an assignment.	We are using data to develop a question to solve.	
Application	We are more comfortable with discrete concepts and skills.	We are applying information to complete an assignment when asked.	We are solving problems by applying knowledge, facts, techniques, or rules in a different way.	
Compassion	We are invested in how we feel about ourselves. We keep to ourselves and generally do not make an effort to understand the feelings of others.	We are friendly to other people and help when they ask.	We are understanding how another person is feeling, and when we see or feel that someone needs help, we look for ways to help him or her.	

Internal Conditions That Support Passionate Learners

	Indifferent	Compliant	Engaged	Passionate
Influencing	We are not invested in getting to know people or issues well enough to have any platform for influence.	We are able to do what we have to do to accomplish a task.	We are understanding when working with others. We follow through with what we say we will do, present ideas, compromise, and build people up by focusing on their strengths.	We are dedicated to our learning and showing it through our commitment. We approach learning through influencing others, our tenacity and perseverance, and creating our own awareness.
Awareness	We are focused on ourselves and have little social awareness.	We are able to reflect on how others might be feeling in a particular situation when asked to do so.	We are able to sense each other's feelings and perceptions.	
Tenacious	We try one way of figuring something out, and if it doesn't work, we find ourselves giving up.	We are able to attempt to figure out another way to accomplish a task or reach a goal if asked to do so.	We are able to stick with a task and figure out additional ways to reach the goal.	
Perseverance	We are finding ourselves giving up early on work, especially when tasks become more difficult.	We are able to continue trying when asked to do so.	We are able to persist on a task until it is complete, even when it becomes challenging.	

CAUTION

- The district, school, or teacher assesses the dispositions on a report card.

  The message sent to students could possibly be that either you have this disposition or you do not have this disposition. How does this leave the student feeling?

- The teacher or parent overvalues an individual skill or disposition either positively or negatively, ultimately resulting in limited composite growth across the dispositions (Barseghian, 2013).

  If the four pillars are not utilized and a disposition is enforced through rewards or punishments, the student may have not truly internalized the disposition.

- Note that dispositions are more difficult to teach "once damaged or extinguished" (Katz, 1993, p. 24)

  The researcher Lillian Katz shares an example of how a disposition can become stronger through proper scaffolds and can weaken if there is not a supportive environment.

Believing that dispositions can make a significant difference in academic and future careers of students, it would be incumbent upon us to look beyond instructional implementation and further investigate the applicability to the full education system such as cocurriculars, developmental guidance models, and parent education. If these areas were strengthened to focus on student engagement and dispositions, the education system would again be working smarter, not harder. Incorporating the dispositions and the Creating Passionate Learners model with relevant and vigorous learning moves students to be truly college, career, and life ready.

Vince Lombardi once said,

To be successful, a man must exert an effective influence upon his brothers and upon his associates, and the degree in which he accomplishes this depends on the personality of the man, the incandescence of which he is capable. The flame of fire that burns inside him. The magnetism which draws the heart of other men to him. (Family of Vince Lombardi, 2010)

The influence people have is connected to the dispositions utilized in their interactions, thoughts, and ideas. The dispositions are the underpinning keys to emotional, behavioral, and cognitive engagement and create the conditions within a person for lifelong learning.

HOW CULTURE SUPPORTS PASSIONATE LEARNERS

Creating a culture and setting a tone for engagement allows for students to learn the skills and strategies to work in the 21st century. When relationships are built and the culture of the classroom is one where students are able to ask questions, take risks, and build upon their strengths, it prepares them to enter the world in which they will contribute. Successful companies are looking for people who will be hands-on contributors, comfortable sharing ideas and opinions, and working within and across teams. When students are given opportunities to work on these skills and strategies within their schooling experiences, they will be prepared to contribute in these same ways in the communities in which they serve.

CHAPTER 7

High–Leverage Reforms

$\mathscr{A}$ teacher whom we have worked with provides a perfect example of the need for a filter to prioritize local initiatives. One teacher shared the following in a survey that was sent prior to the start of the strategic planning process: "I never understood what the vision was. From my viewpoint, every initiative appeared important. By focusing on many initiatives, in reality, we never really focused on any. In the end, it just felt like confusion."

Districts benefit from narrowing their initiative focus. This district had a leadership team that was quite informed and very well intended. They were strong researchers and had developed expertise in a variety of best practices. Collectively, they did not see an improvement initiative they didn't like. Their goal appeared to be positioned to say, "We are doing it all." The problem became very noticeable as the scope creep in the improvement work began to compound. The further down the path any one of the initiatives progressed, there was a lack of fidelity of practice and a tremendous variety of practice. Initially, questions were raised. Even among early adopters, dissent emerged. As time went on, with additional mandates and optional implementation strategies mounting, followers became discouraged. Early adopters joined the remaining faculty in becoming one body working against the will of the district office.

The district took action by holding faculty listening sessions where concerns were outlined and validated. Based on that faculty feedback, a conscious choice by the administration was made to prioritize initiatives focused on student engagement. Therefore, through listening and collaboration, the district regained focus and faculty again engaged in work they saw as meaningful. The beliefs from the Framework for Creating Passionate Learners (Figure 7.1)—the confluence of growth mindset, internal dialogue, self-determination, and culture—served as the actual filter causing the faculty to prioritize work they chose as meaningful.

Nationwide, the current landscape could be described as a revolution in education. The revolution is evidenced by current scrutiny on resources, expectations, political attention, and accountability, including school report cards and large-scale assessment models. This landscape has resulted in silver-bullet remedies that leave one feeling overwhelmed, confused, and exhausted. In this context, reformers abound. Three types of reformers are accountability driven, initiative driven, and accomplished reformers. Figure 7.2 thoroughly describes each of these reformer types.

We argue that accomplished reformers get more respect from followers. Reformers who are accountability driven will cause a

Figure 7.1 Beliefs

Figure 7.2 Reformer Types

Types of Reformers	Accountability Driven	Initiative Driven	Accomplished Reformer
Characteristics present	Measuring, ranking, and sorting	Believing every new process has value—let's do them all	Truly student centered
Examples	Large-scale assessment, school report card, educator effectiveness, and pay for performance	Embracing each new initiative, taking none to the implementation level desired	Student as customer
Rationale why I am doing this	Measurements for things that matter	Capacity as abundant—we can do it all! Bring us some more! Making connections is not a priority	Engaged, lifelong learners

transactional change only. The hallmark of transactional change is that there are new processes and procedures to complete, but the underlying beliefs and core skills that were utilized in the past remain unchanged (Frontier & Rickabaugh, 2015). The reformer's goal is to make change that moves beyond new processes and programs for adults and ensures new, more engaging learning experiences for students. Actions from some leaders may get results, but in many cases, those results don't last. Reformers who are initiative driven are well intended, work hard, and will get limited results. Initiative-driven reformers may find that anticipated results actually fall short. The type of reformer who can leverage student inspiration is the accomplished reformer (Frontier & Rickabaugh, 2014).

STUDENT ENGAGEMENT AS THE FILTER FOR HIGH-LEVERAGE REFORM

A student engagement filter for reform intentionally causes some different conversations to take place that should take place. Tony Frontier and Jim Rickabaugh (2014) share key questions that one needs to ask in order to make transformational change occur in a manner that students notice. A question such as the following can take conversations to a deeper level, to empower all stakeholders to focus on the right work: "How will students be engaged with adults in developing their learning path?" (Frontier & Rickabaugh, 2014, p. 173).

The power in student engagement being the filter for reform is phenomenal. No longer are we going one-to-one in technology because the neighboring district is. No longer should the pressures of interest groups drive decisions on initiatives. We still may be forced to do things that others have directed but can decide where they fit in our improvement plan. In the case studies below, we give examples of reforms that are transactional and reforms that are transformative in nature, selected for their student-centered benefit. The first transformational example focuses on continuous improvement.

Our second transformational example, on community-based learning (CBL; Prast & Viegut, 2014), is defined as an intentional marriage between best practices and advocacy for education by jointly conceiving rigorous, vigorous, relevant learning experiences for students. CBL, in its richest form, is mindful of what preparation students really need to be college, career, and life ready and may take place in a variety of settings throughout communities.

CASE STUDIES: TRANSACTIONAL AND TRANSFORMATIONAL

Case 1: A Transactional Example

One district was made aware that a number of schools were striving to use a continuous improvement model. Thinking this was central to their work, they began with efforts in training many staff members who were willing to devote a week of their summer to the initiative. The teachers and administrators who volunteered to be trained learned strategies that they could use to engage their students and teachers in the learning process. A smattering of classrooms across the district utilized some of the strategies and saw the benefits of giving students ownership in their learning, while at the same time, the knowledge base and conversations in other classrooms and buildings went unchanged. Unfortunately, a key piece that was missing was involving the students in the change process.

The district utilized some improvement strategies but failed to employ a system that included student voice and struggled to determine why the organization was not making an impact at the classroom level. The improvement plan was set in motion, but when it came to reflecting on progress, only administration was at the table; key voices were missing from the conversation.

Money was spent for continued training for a few key teacher leaders in the district, but there was not a plan to intentionally infiltrate other classrooms. The work made some progress; however, the most noticeable void was that the approach never got students to internalize the importance of the work to them. Through the lens of the students, they were not engaged. The implementation plan failed on a number of key issues: influencing student passion, developing their own life skills, and institutionally reaching all teachers and classrooms.

Case 1: A Transformational Example

The Menomonee Falls School District in Wisconsin is being recognized internationally for their work on continuous improvement.

It is one of the best examples of a systems-driven, student-engaged improvement practice. Continuous improvement, done well, defines the right behaviors and roots out the poor behaviors at every level of the organization from the board of education to individual kindergarten students. In the classroom improvement process at Menomonee Falls, feedback loops between teachers and students have grown to be expected and are commonplace. You routinely will see the littlest kids sharing with the teacher what they need to learn next.

Student internal dialogue and metacognition are driving forces to the improvement process PK–12. Teachers and students alike model the growth mindset necessary to get to mastery. Curiosity, intrigue, risk taking, and being assertive are commonplace. This is an example where student engagement in the process was a filter on the front end of the decision to engage continuous improvement. Furthermore, the skills the students are learning, developing, and gaining mastery at are the same skills that their local business community is expecting of their adults.

The superintendent, Dr. Pat Greco, was mindful about how each person in the organization was trained and redefined administrator priorities and the instructional coach's position to focus on modeling the strategies.

Case 2: A Transactional Example

Seeing community involvement in learning increasing as a practice, one building decided to work with a local business partner. With great intentions, each looked at how they could benefit one another. A field trip was planned for the upper elementary students to visit the local business and learn the different aspects of work as well as what skills and preparation they would need to work there. The business partner enjoyed the student visit. In return, they requested that the students return over the holiday and sing for the employees during the lunch hour. The gracious business partner organized a luncheon for all students.

Although the experience was memorable, and some learning did take place, it did not directly relate to the curriculum, students did not own any part of the passive experience, and the experience did not endure beyond that day. Upon further analysis, something even more troubling was present. Every school experience takes time, and time is a precious commodity in schools as well as in the lives of our business partners. When the singing and lunch were over, the partners on both sides felt as though they had just collaborated on a great project. These types of experiences can be great starting points that lead to strengthened and more valuable experiences; however, when they result in partners feeling done, could the time have been better spent? Are the students getting the rigor, vigor, and relevance needed for their preparation? Do business partners leave these experiences with low confidence in the ability of public education to do what is deemed as really important?

Case 2: A Transformational Example

When a group of teachers were introduced to the concept of Community Based Learners (CBL) and had internalized the mutual benefits to students and emerging partnerships, they immediately began planning how they could bring this reform to life. The belief system of the group was that all students can learn better in a community-based setting of greater rigor and relevance. To do this, the teachers decided a transformation was needed. Their mission was to better engage students and create a sense of community through partnering on content, delivery, and mutual outcomes.

Using a project-based model and a renewed emphasis on partnering with the community and curricular standards, educators and community members joined in the design on how they could better inspire students. As all stakeholders internalized the benefits to students, educators and community members alike could see the support for the community-based approach in education grow. What resulted was a context where students were mastering how to truly become college, career, and life ready.

Students researched topics so that issues were understood holistically in order to take action. They then took their research on the topics and found ways to advocate, increase awareness, promote philanthropy, or serve their community. Student actions in these community partnerships resulted in increased student motivation and deeper learning and also made a difference in some aspect of community life. The experience culminated in student presentations to authentic audiences. Students practiced their presentations in front of community volunteers, further extending their community learning to even more audiences. This feedback was invaluable as students prepared for their formal (summative) presentations to the community.

After the community project was carried out, students gathered in seminar to learn additional essential concepts from the experiences of fellow students. During seminar, students had the opportunity to self-direct their next learning as well as experience another level of direct instruction related to the curriculum. Students then reflected on their learning, which guided the teachers' next steps the following day.

The teachers were mindful of the language they used with their students so that students felt empowered. The culture of a CBL classroom is one in which students sense the camaraderie to make a difference in their community and the lives of others as well as themselves.

In the preceding examples, being mindful of the Framework for Creating Passionate Learners as a filter for reform serves leaders and reformers well. What can begin as well intended, with great energy and expectation, can end up falling far short, ultimately resulting in frustration. Using the Framework for Creating Passionate Learners as the filter for reform changes beliefs, strategies, and outcomes for reform efforts. Students want to be challenged and engaged; when reforms don't allow for that, it should not be surprising that students don't see the value in what was intended.

School leaders are faced with an overabundance of proposed solutions targeted at every problem facing education today. Every challenge we face, including facilities, school safety, the instructional system, and branding, has a vendor claiming to have the answer school leaders need. In actuality, what is needed is a filter to help us discern which of these reforms has the greatest possibility of inspiring students and achieving preferred results.

CONSIDERATIONS AND IMPLICATIONS IN DETERMINING HIGH-LEVERAGE REFORM STRATEGIES

Internalizing the differences between low-level versus high-level reform, one can quickly see the impact on students. Low-level reform perpetuates the current decline in student engagement. In contrast, high-level reform, with student engagement central to the mission of the reform, matters to students.

Once a discriminating eye for high-leverage reform is developed, a process will be necessary to move from divergent possibilities to actionable steps that are a good bet—a good bet because of the focus on growth mindset, internal dialogue, self-determination, and culture. Figure 7.3 suggests a process to support that work.

We live and work in this most interesting time in history and in the history of our profession of education. Confusion and paralysis are alive in too many of us, in part driven by the landscape changes in the economy, politics, and perceptions of education. This landscape of scrutiny, initiatives, and accountability, as we have come to know, may not likely change or lessen in our near future. We can look at the tension present and the initiative overloads and think, "Poor us." Or, we can say, "What an opportunity we have been presented!" Our own growth mindset is a necessary driver right now, for this is a time of influence for the informed and eager.

In this time of challenge in our profession, we offer a sound solution. We must understand this context and landscape intimately, understand what is driving the accountability- and initiative-laden industry, understand the Framework for Creating Passionate Learners, and use that framework as a filter for developing or choosing high-leverage reform strategies. This approach of using the Framework of Creating Passionate Learners for filtering

Figure 7.3   A Suggested Process for Determining a High-Leverage Reform

School leaders conduct a broad assessment of organizational practice and make conscious choices to focus on student engagement.
School leaders analyze results from engagement assessments to determine direction.
School leaders consider a divergent review of student-focused reform options.
School leaders narrow the scope of possibilities based upon impact on student engagement.
School leaders select a reform strategy while being mindful of creating passionate learners.
School leaders establish goals and define a starting point.

high-leverage reform has a far greater potential of ensuring a future that is student centered over a future driven by initiatives, accountability, or worse—someone's pet project. In the most simple of forms, a basic, yet effective filter strategy is to do as author Tony Frontier (2014) has stated: "If all the mandates dried up, what is so important to students that we would still choose to hang on to? What makes an idea/strategy worthy of continuing to spend time on?"

The excitement for the education community results in a renewed sense of intrinsic motivation from educators and students alike. Being mindful of the current level of student disengagement, resulting in part from the initiative and accountability era, has served as energy for the work on *Creating Passionate Learners.* The authors have intentionally created an argument and system to reinspire leaders, faculty, and learners. Stakeholders in the education system, connecting to the message in this book, will create conditions where we work smarter, not harder. Inspiring a new population of learners to be passionate about their learning is clearly a working smarter strategy. We learn more and better when we undergo an experience that leads to personal passion and engagement (Dewey, 1937). Indeed, we have an incredible opportunity to change the industry and ultimately and significantly to enhance student passion.

CHAPTER 8

Leading the Transformation for Creating Passionate Learners

The 1970s were a place and time where strong school managers were hired and appreciated. This was a cohort of people who were appreciated for working hard, long days, managing student behavior, and stabilizing a comprehensive suite of educational opportunities that was to result in well-rounded young men and women.

Throughout the next 30 years, the school management emphasis became viewed as a basic leader expectation so that persons who held school administrative positions could transition their focus to leading instruction. During this period in time, to some, an overemphasis on large-scale assessment resulted in framing the expectations and actions of instructional leaders. Work such as aligning to assessed standards, planning for and administering large-scale assessments, group data retreats, and faculty meetings focused on responding to results were examples of what leading instruction looked like.

At the same time there was a serious evolution underway in the traits, abilities, experiences, and expectations of who was to be hired as the next cohort of school leaders. Teachers who demonstrated proficiency in core content, instructional effectiveness, use of data and who were contributing members of school improvement planning teams had advantages when applying to be the next school leaders. Great progress was made in more clearly understanding content standards, scaffolding learning targets across the grades, using data to inform instruction, intervention and programming, and written plans for professional development and improvement planning. Perhaps an area that was not emphasized enough was a focus on student engagement. The majority of the actions in education at this time happened to the students—students did not have a voice.

Progress was being made, however, not at the pace that satisfied critics and reformers alike. The period in time that was focused on leading instruction was a time where systems, structures, and initiatives were researched, tried, and implemented in response to the call to action to improve student learning. Many of these well-intended systems and structures actually resulted in eventually being in the way of actions that inspired learners. The educational managers of the 1970s and the instructional leaders during the years that followed were good people who worked hard and wanted to do the right things for their schools. Missing throughout this time was a full institutional focus on learners themselves, more specifically a leader focus on inspiring students to be equipped to develop themselves into passionate learners.

The next generation of focus for school leaders must be to shift the work to student engagement (Schlechty, 1997). Leader actions and the energy of their organizations must move directly to student passion and the knowledge necessary to enable creating inspired, self-motivated learners. Leaders can cause students to see themselves as engaged, motivated, and able to learn. Prioritizing leader's work around student engagement is essential.

To illustrate this concept further, Table 8.1 offers a comparison on leader work that is not mindful of student engagement and, conversely, that same work as mindful of creating passionate learners.

The examples in Tables 8.1 and 8.2 are either mindful or not mindful of creating passionate learners. The intended outcomes are dependent upon commitment to changing students' engagement

Table 8.1   Focus on Student Engagement

Characteristics of Not Being Mindful of Creating Passionate Learners	Characteristics of Being Mindful of Creating Passionate Learners
The focus in school improvement plans emphasizes the initiatives currently underway.	Teacher dispositions, skills, and internal conditions are given attention.
Feedback, when visible, is given one way only—teacher to students. Feedback loops are not thought of. Feedback does not include vocabulary from the Framework for Creating Passionate Learners.	Staff and students are taught the Framework for Creating Passionate Learners (cognitive).
Progress monitoring focuses solely on academic growth; student dispositions are not considered.	Student status in dispositions, skills, internal conditions, and overall engagement is monitored and known by students (behavioral).
Intervention plans focus solely on bottom-line academic growth.	Teachers' feedback is mindful of words and actions relative to individual student status (emotional).
Administrator evaluations emphasize the cosmetic nature of improvement plans.	Culture and context are studied, inform dialogue and actions, and inspire student motivation (emotional).
Data retreats are held. Subsequent professional development plans reflect the academic shortcomings uncovered. Student engagement is not central to the data retreat.	Community partnerships create awareness of the Framework for Creating Passionate Learners, resulting in a common vocabulary (behavioral).
Attention is not given to student voice.	The Framework for Creating Passionate Learners is alive in conversations and choices made in what to teach, how to teach, how to assess, and how data inform interactions (emotional).
Dialogue with students doesn't appear to have changed over time.	The connection to rigorous, vigorous, and relevant learning choices is clear and routine (cognitive and behavioral).
When asked, students would say they comply; however, school is something that happens to them.	Principals routinely check in with faculty and focus on student engagement status (emotional).
	Student-led conferences focus on achievement and student engagement status as mutually inclusive (emotional, behavioral, and cognitive).
	Administrators and teachers are visibly having very different, intentional conversations with students, listening to the students' ideas and needs (emotional, behavioral, and cognitive).

Table 8.2   Governing and Leading Coherently

A Superintendent Less Mindful of Creating Passionate Learners	A Superintendent Who Is Mindful of Creating Passionate Learners
The board works hard, holds many meetings, even attends school functions; however, student issues and needs are rarely discussed in board meetings. Student involvement in what has historically been the business of the adults is limited or nonexistent. Students are not invited into discussions regarding site improvement planning. Those plans happen to the students. The board and superintendent appear unaware of the research-based best practice related to creating passionate learners. Resources dedicated to student engagement are not considered. Work on policies, finances, personnel, and crises squeeze out space for focusing on student engagement.	The board and superintendent are routinely seen discussing students' interests, needs, and voice. Students are included in improvement planning. The board has become knowledgeable regarding the framework for creating passionate learners, and their own use of the common vocabulary is visible. Resources are allocated annually based upon student engagement. Board members' questions and dialogue clearly have shifted; for example, how will this initiative impact student motivation?

status. Filtering leader's actions through the Framework for Creating Passionate Learners results in mindfulness and a very different dialogue with our learners.

PLANNING FOR TRANSFORMATIONAL CHANGE AND THE SYSTEM WORK OF SCHOOL LEADERS

Leaders are faced with demands and choices in their daily system work. Transformational leaders embrace others in school improvement planning. Transformational leaders do a thoughtful review of divergent possibilities and choose a direction with the greatest probability of inspiring students. Transformational leaders work to promote student engagement in existing efforts linking curriculum, instruction, assessment, and intervention.

Transformational leaders calendar the work through a sequence of research, planning, piloting, and program assessment and eventually plan to take the start-up work to scale.

Transformational leaders facilitate leaders of the faculty. In the eyes of faculty, transformational leaders are fully present, in the moment, and are seen talking about students and student engagement. Transformational leaders use valuable face-to-face time with faculty for meaningful, student-centered work. The faculty see transformational leaders as willing to invest in them, valuing learning among the adults. Faculty know their voice and involvement are valued and welcome, which results in routine opportunities for deep dialogue. Transformational leaders believe in creating a culture of innovation, trust, and improvement where distributive leadership is present.

Transformational leaders analyze important data and coordinate subsequent professional development opportunities. Transformation leaders establish reliability data systems that include teacher and student engagement status. Faculty have full knowledge that the transformational leader conducts short-cycle assessments so that program adjustments lead to quality improvements. Transformational leaders ensure improvement discussions take place at every level within the organization so that all employees see the vision and data and can help inform next steps. Professional learning plans are truly student centered. Leadership and educator development are clearly linked to increasing student engagement. The transformational change strategies in Figure 8.1 include an emphasis on creating passionate learners and can be used to guide leader thinking and actions.

Figure 8.1   Transformational Change Planning Strategies

Leaders scope out the context for its emphasis on creating passionate learners.	Leaders stage for success in their efforts to strengthen district pro-action on student engagement.	Leaders engage stakeholders to drive their commitment to creating passionate learners.	Leaders enact transform-ational change with confidence in improving student engagement.	Leaders sustain the change while championing increases in students recognized as passionate learners.

The suggestions in Figure 8.1 will garner a following and leverage the kind of transformational change students need. In transformational change, the underlying beliefs on important work are evolving, and the intent and action are recognizable by students.

TRANSFORMATIONAL LEADERSHIP IN ACTION

Quint Studer, author, leader, and reformer in the health care and education arenas, has published numerous books focused on improving systems and the people that work in those systems. Studer's work in evidence-based leadership outlines specific beliefs and actions that if employed with fidelity, simply get results. Studer defines a list of principles that serves as the anchor for his improvement work. For the sake of discussion related to creating passionate learners, let's focus on the first two principles in Studer's (2003) work:

- Commit to excellence.
- Measure the important things.

> Excellence is when leadership and employee satisfaction are created and sustained through a culture of service and operational efficiency (Studer, 2003). Studer associates Janet Pilcher and Robin Largue (2009), in their book *How to Lead Teachers to Become Great*, say that "what teacher's measure, student's value" (p. 59).

Being vague about excellence hurts our credibility and our cause. One example of a leader's action where being vague works against progress would be leaders simply saying we commit to excellence without defining excellence. Defining excellence and then committing to that definition are essential to raising expectations clearly for followers. When we are mindful of the Framework for Creating Passionate Learners and how that related work can transcend to the major aspects of the instructional system, our definition of excellence changes. Stakeholder perception of what we are committing to becomes clearer, and engagement on the part of the adults becomes more probable. Leaders of the future must strongly state that creating passionate learners is central to our definition of excellence and commit to that definition.

Transformational leaders inspire teachers to make a deeper impact on student learning. In turn, teachers also play significant transformational roles in inspiring student engagement. Key is the teachers' knowledge of student status in behavioral, emotional, and cognitive influences. A variety of tools are available to measure student engagement status. By measuring individual engagement status and establishing specific goals and actionable steps, we are increasing students' perceived value of the energy needed to improve their engagement status. A variety of tools are available to measure student engagement status. Our recommendation is to use the survey tool developed by coauthor Tony Frontier (2007). The survey questions on this tool delve deep into the behavioral, emotional, and cognitive status of individual learners. Here is a sampling of those survey items:

1. In my classes, I need to think creatively (cognitive).

2. In my classes, I am allowed to make choices about projects I do or what I learn (behavioral).

3. My teachers are interested in my thoughts and opinions (emotional).

The survey is directly linked to the Framework for Creating Passionate Learners. The results are to inform practice and enhance student engagement. For access to the full survey, contact Tony Frontier, acfrontier@stritch.edu.

Having and using the data just discussed are essential. However, those actions alone are not enough. Just as with any successful endeavor, a deeper systems look is required that further supports needs the teachers have in the classroom. The following sections of this chapter suggest specific actions for building- and district-level leaders, suggestions that actually fit both roles and provide the necessary support.

INFLUENCING A HEIGHTENED LEADER COMMITMENT TO STUDENT ENGAGEMENT

Building Level

Building-level leaders are faced with many choices in how to spend their days. Prioritizing those choices around actions most impactful to improvement is critical. Furthermore, determining how those priorities result in actions that best engage students will shape leader work for the future, specifically, the actions of building principals in the areas of mindset, internal dialogue, self-determination, and culture.

Principals who understand and value mindset emphasize it as they go about their work. These leaders are completely aware of the importance of teaching students about growth mindset and creating a culture of effort between and among teachers and students alike. These leaders create opportunities for faculty to assess their mindsets, discuss moving their own mindsets to a growth mindset and modeling that for students. Through think alouds, they share their internal messages and how they are changing those internal messages in a positive way. Through regular faculty meetings and one-on-one conferring, principals can both model their expectations and assist faculty in ensuring that student understanding and status of mindset are monitored and adjustments are routinely made.

Focusing on internal dialogue requires principals to get all hands on deck. All stakeholders need to understand the importance and impact of feedback, the words we choose to use with students, and the impact of those words. When students, in their gut, say to themselves, "I can do this; I need to learn this; I need to drive my actions for my future; *self-directing my learning is completely up to me,*" it is then that the students have internalized the importance of why their self-talk matters, and then they can direct their self-talk to be positive.

In addition, principals whose observations focus on teacher feedback can bring a heightened awareness to the type of feedback teachers give most often in a typical lesson. When principals share the data they gather on feedback, and give time for the teachers to reflect upon it and to practice collaboratively giving data- and inquiry-based feedback, internal dialogue can be enhanced.

Principals who work with faculty to internalize and act upon self-determination are taking the right steps to model this important condition for students. Progress in self-determination must begin with teachers understanding why giving students autonomy and ownership is vitally important to students directing their own achievement. Principals who work side by side with teachers to determine current levels of student engagement and commit to increasing that engagement understand that autonomous learners are better-engaged learners. They further understand that students who take ownership in their learning are better-engaged learners. Principals who support increasing teacher capacity in seeing students as autonomous learners and teacher actions that increase ownership stand a far greater chance of changing student perceptions of who autonomous-supportive teachers are.

Culture captures a composite of who and what we are as a collective learning environment. Principals aware of the need to tend to culture because of the impact on student engagement lead faculty in ways visible to students. Culture is the ultimate result of mindset, internal dialogue, and self-determination. In a recent presentation on student engagement, one principal followed the discussion by stating that his first step in creating that culture would be to get to know every student better by name, background, and interests. Building upon his good start would be the suggestion to do the same with each staff member. A culture where learning is expected and supported and the conditions of mindset, internal dialogue, and self-determination are visible to staff and students alike is a culture that transforms learning as a result of students being far more engaged. A 21st-century building leader transforms the learning culture for students to become truly engaged.

School improvement planning that has student engagement central to that plan focuses on necessary student support structures so that improved student engagement is a priority and can be realized. More specifically, many existing improvement plans have a focus on math and literacy. Leaders who work to improve achievement and address the gap with a plan filtered through the work of creating passionate learners stand a greater chance to better engage learners (Quaglia, personal communication, 2014).

For example, reflect on a current goal you may be working on in math or literacy. By embedding an early action step from the Framework for Creating Passionate Learners, such as internal dialogue, leaders are influencing beliefs and strengthening goals.

Building-level instructional leaders need to be mindful of creating passionate learners. Student engagement is central to their work, to their thinking and decisions, and to their actions in numerous ways.

Seven Steps Principals Can Take to Create Passionate Learners

1. Large-Scale Assessment: Appropriate time on task and other measures can provide more accurate predictions of results.

2. School Improvement Planning: Plans are filtered through a lens of student engagement.

3. Professional Development Plans: Regardless of the change in initiative, student engagement remains the primary focus in each endeavor.

4. Data Digs: Data on student engagement is routinely correlated to achievement data.

5. Educator Evaluation: Expectations, observations, and feedback focus on student engagement. For example, if your educator evaluation model is the Framework for Teaching by Charlotte Danielson, getting to a Level 4 must encompass the four central tenants in the Framework for Creating Passionate Learners. The expectation at Level 4 is for students to take more ownership in the learning process. In addition, the expectation is for teachers to use words that are intentional in positive feedback that moves students forward in their learning.

6. Progress Monitoring: Student engagement is central to routine progress monitoring.

7. Professional Learning Communities (PLCs): Improving student engagement is central to the research, discussions, and actions of the PLC.

DANIELSON'S FRAMEWORK FOR TEACHING

The Framework for Teaching is a research-based set of components created by Charlotte Danielson as a means to have reflective discussions with educators about effective teaching practices. The framework is made up of 22 components divided into four domains with the rubric ranging between Levels 1 and 4.

An appropriate building emphasis must be placed on student engagement. Progress in our improvement work may be evident; however, if we miss our focus on student engagement or underemphasize it, will we not move the needle enough for individual kids. A commitment to true student-centered leadership focused on student engagement is necessary. Sarah Martin, a principal at Stonefields School in Auckland, Finland, has an intense building focus on student engagement. Martin shared these key questions that every adult in the school should ask: "Would your kids turn up for school if they didn't have to?" "What would they turn up for?" "What do we keep doing?" "What do we need to stop?" (Martin, 2014). The author's position is to filter each future leader action and initiative through engagement literacy.

Leaders should have a heightened focus on more humanistic leadership that continues efforts of enhancing teaching and learning while at the same time focusing on changing lives. Changing internal dialogue has the potential to change teaching, learning, and the lives of our students. Leaders mindful of a very different dialogue needed with students are intentional about expecting and modeling a dialogue that inspires engagement.

District Level

Similar to building-level leaders, district-level leaders face an uncommon volume of work while at the same time navigating a landscape rich in tension and scrutiny. Prioritizing that volume is essential to personal and organizational success. At the same time, prioritizing helps leaders better navigate the tensions of our current landscape. Additionally, enhancing the priorities through a focus on student engagement demonstrates a preferred future.

District leaders knowledgeable of the need to further engage learners will focus the organization on the four internal conditions of mindset, internal dialogue, self-determination, and culture. Believing in the importance of the work on mindset, district-level leaders shape the work and future of the school districts by defined actions. They first are seen as learners of the Framework for Creating Passionate Learners and reflect on how to best maneuver this work through the existing system. They further their actions by expecting this learning of those immediately around them, creating a buzz about the possibilities and impact on students. They assess the levers they know have the greatest influence in moving issues through the system and begin to deploy strategies that have worked for them in the past. Strategies such as conversations with building leaders, faculty leaders, and the board of education to create the want for goals to be established, resources to be aligned, professional learning plans to be adopted, and the systems work to be done is then calendared out.

Emphasizing learning about mindset and expecting building-level leaders to focus on mindset may increase the number of students who have growth mindsets. Informed district-level leaders know that students with growth mindsets exert more effort and perform better than students with fixed mindsets, ultimately impacting students having entirely different views of themselves, their learning, and lives.

Also needing attention at the district level is a focus on internal dialogue. Recalling a time when a group of principals were involved in a book study on choice words, some of the principals laughed and saw the book as a boring read. Some of them didn't get it! Nesting that important conversation in the Framework for Creating Passionate Learners causes a far different reaction. People say that the language each person in an organization uses matters and is just common sense; why have we not always done this?

District leaders have so much authority to decide direction and program emphasis. Regarding internal dialogue, district leaders can expect that people give feedback to one another with the same words they use with students. They can support adult learning plans that emphasize deeper understanding of feedback that leads to metacognition. District-level leaders need to share the goal that the organization intends to monitor adult attention toward dialogue impacting staff and students alike. District-level leaders should develop tools to have its stakeholders self-assess and create opportunities for reflection. They can help set goals for the organization and continue to focus on those goals; however, it is ultimately conversations with the stakeholders that create the energy to change the organization. We know that the stakeholders have to believe in things like internal dialogue wholeheartedly for students to realize the end benefit.

Ownership and autonomy are key in self-determination. When individuals perceive that they are being listened and responded to, they feel their needs are being met and, thus, are more intrinsically motivated, leading to being more engaged in their work or learning. Most of us as adult workers prefer to be provided with autonomous work settings as well, along with autonomous support from our peers and supervisors. District-level leaders identify with self-determination, as most have grown to see that condition as central to success. Creating a work setting where autonomous support is modeled from the district level sets the stage for all adults to see this condition as a benefit for students as well.

Purpose, commitment, and trust are important in culture. District-level leaders must value and nurture cultures where students are inspired, engaged, and successful. District-level leaders can support this work by highlighting case studies where an emphasis on culture results in improved student engagement. A conscious effort can be made by district leaders to have principals showcase examples of classroom cultures that have evolved to the point of students mutually supporting the learning of fellow classmates. Cultures inclusive of growth mindset, internal dialogue, and self-determination will focus directly on creating passionate learners.

Actions of district-level leaders demonstrate how their priority work takes a deeper meaning while at the same time causing the entire organization to focus its work through the lens of engaged learners.

Five Steps District-Level Leaders Can Take to Create Passionate Learners

1. Intentionally establish personal learning plans on the subject of creating passionate learners for the purpose of informing future discussions and actions. Book studies, professional development conferences, and inquiries with faculty are suggested starting points.

2. Understand that a transformative culture will be necessary to cause needed change, specifically, a culture around the four beliefs of creating passionate learners.

3. Once informed on the merits of creating passionate learners, expect that student engagement becomes central to district and building beliefs, plans, committee work, data reviews, progress monitoring, and reporting. This level of focus will move the cause to become institutional and increase the probability of the work being sustained.

4. Dedicate district, building, and classroom budgets to enhance student engagement. Stakeholders see greater value in priorities that have resources linked to their research and implementation. Book studies, planning time related to creating passionate learners, and teacher time for collaborative coworker observation and coaching are examples of creating the conditions for success through allocation of resources.

5. Reinforce teacher efforts by making visible the work of the superintendent and board of education (Schlechty, 1997) on student engagement. Teachers observe and are aware of what the superintendent and board are talking about when they are together. When board agenda items, board visits, and board talking points within the community reflect what teachers are valuing in student engagement, all stakeholders begin to feel as though they are part of something bigger than themselves.

Seven Steps Both Principals and District
Leaders Can Take to Create Passionate Learners

1. Develop an understanding in the leaders and teachers in your organization about the rationale for the Framework for Creating Passionate Learners. An example of a sustained professional development plan for creating passionate learners simply would be an annual calendar of work that represents a plan of learning progress for the adults.

2. Create a common vocabulary within the education community, with the greater community, and with parents regarding the rationale, strategies for development, feedback, outcomes, and common messaging for creating passionate learners.

3. Leverage community resources to aide in the messaging of creating passionate learners to cause a multiplying effect. When students routinely see business and community partners valuing and reinforcing the essential work of schools, students see greater value in everyone's efforts to develop necessary lifelong skills.

4. Monitor improvement data, and query the correlation attributed to the Framework for Creating Passionate Learners for improved outcomes. This effort moves the discussion from what the data alone are saying to a more complete cause-and-effect conversation.

5. Assess organizational practice to ensure the Framework for Creating Passionate Learners is given appropriate attention.

Here is an opportunity to further explore the ideas that have been discussed regarding building- and district-level leader actions. In Table 8.3, in the left column are identifiable and routine building- or district-level leader actions such as Educator Effectiveness,

Table 8.3   Work Through the Lens of Creating Passionate Learners

Priority Actions of Leaders	Enhancing the Priorities
Leader Initiative	How a leader's work is enhanced when the work is viewed through a lens of the Framework for Creating Passionate Learners.
Educator Effectiveness	Students have voice and choice in the classroom. Students are involved in self-reflection in both achievement gaps as well as growth targets in the Framework for Creating Passionate Learners. A heightened dialogue exists among all stakeholders on dispositions.
School Improvement Planning	Student engagement drives priorities and actions in school improvement work and influences adult time on task. Students understand the goal and are invited into efforts toward that goal or solution.
Professional Learning Communities	Teacher discussions in collaborative analysis of student work are anchored in the conceptual Framework for Creating Passionate Learners.

School Improvement Planning, and Professional Learning Communities, and in the right column is listed an example of how that work is enhanced when viewed through a lens of the Framework for Creating Passionate Learners.

In the space provided in the left-hand column in Table 8.4, list additional priority actions of a leader, and in the right-hand column, describe how that work could be enhanced when viewed through the lens of the Framework for Creating Passionate Learners.

GUIDING LEADERS' FOCUS ON STUDENT ENGAGEMENT

The initiatives administrators choose to lead should be filtered through student engagement to determine the level of attention the organization intends to devote to that work. Following this type of filtering exercise, school leaders quickly will see if our intended actions matter to the learners or, worse, are another thing that lay in the way of student motivation, actually keeping them from mastery. The statements in Table 8.5 are essential in assisting leader focus.

As was discussed previously, leaders have an abundance of choices that drive their daily work. Narrowing that focus to the priorities that have the greatest probability of causing transformational change has never been more important. Student engagement clearly is one of those priorities. Leaders, though, cannot fall into the trap of simple compliance to engagement issues that may have less meaning

Table 8.4   Working Through the Lens of the Framework for Creating Passionate Learners in Your School

Priority Actions of Leaders	Enhancing the Priorities

Table 8.5   Filter for Student Engagement

Absent	Emerging	Accomplished
1. The school community and the greater community share a common vocabulary on student engagement.		
A common vocabulary on creating passionate learners and student engagement does not exist.	The education community has begun to research and has pockets of implementation; however, the community at large is unaware of the initiative or effort.	The education community and the community at large speak to student engagement through growth mindset, internal dialogue, self-determination, and culture.
2. Student engagement as a part of the leader's evaluation.		
Engagement is not currently considered.	There is compliance to external mandates.	The community expects the leader to emphasize the beliefs outlined in the Framework for Creating Passionate Learners.
3. Student engagement is explicit in professional development, district, building, and individual plans.		
Professional development is compliant with external mandates at best.	Professional development plans exist, are coherent, but the link to student engagement is unclear.	Professional development plans are anchored in student engagement status.
4. Student engagement is central to expectations and feedback on educator evaluation.		
Educator evaluation activities center on the mechanics of implementation.	Discussions are unfolding linking high instructional effectiveness to student engagement.	Student engagement is the filter for all educator evaluation discussions and decisions.
5. Leaders intentionally invest in staff and in student engagement.		
Resources are distributed absent a coherent plan.	On a growing basis, current resource allocation is questioned, and priorities are being reestablished.	District and site resources are prioritized and allocated based on student engagement status.

Absent	Emerging	Accomplished
6. Teacher collaboration time is provided and focused in a larger part on student engagement.		
Teacher collaboration on priority work is not valued; initiatives happen to teachers.	Early adopters are reaching out to coworkers.	Teacher leaders drive the existing culture of innovation and improvement based on engagement status.
7. Learner profiles are utilized, and engagement status is acted upon.		
Learner profiles do not exist.	Learner profiles exist and are used in pockets of practice; meaningful profiles are misunderstood.	Acting on emotional, behavioral, and cognitive student engagement status, from the learner profile, is standard operating procedure.
8. The district's continuous improvement plan is influenced by current research and practice relative to student engagement.		
Vision, decisions, and actions around school improvement planning are difficult to find.	School improvement plans exist; however, the primary focus remains on systems and structures.	School improvement decisions are filtered through growth mindset, internal dialogue, self-determination, and culture.
9. Board of education time on task focuses on student engagement.		
Long board meetings exist; however, they are occupied with operational discussions.	Board discussions are underway, and student engagement surfaces in those discussions; however, even those closest to the work struggle to link those discussions to their real work.	The board as a whole monitors strategies in growth mindset, internal dialogue, self-determination, and culture and works with administration on adjusting efforts based on results.
10. Employees are committed to their own personal growth and transformation and see the correlation to improving student engagement status.		
Personal improvement, personal	Successful people and districts are being researched. The gap	Employees make connections between their growth mindsets, their internal dialogues,

(Continued)

Table 8.5 (Continued)

Absent	Emerging	Accomplished
transformation, and individual growth among adults is viewed as something as good for someone else to do. Neither personal transformation nor student engagement is on the radar.	between current practice and preferred practice is researched. Plans are underway to achieve their same success. The correlation between personal transformation and student engagement is emerging.	their self-determination, and their culture and their impact on the same for students.

such as attendance, graduation rates, and discipline records. The leader's obligation is to ensure the dialogue focuses on emotional engagement, behavioral engagement, and cognitive engagement as essential to improving learning for individual students.

Leaders need to know the importance of a focus on student engagement and also know the status of student engagement in their own settings. The leader also needs to shape the system's lens so that all of the related variables are identified, considered, and acted upon. The following questions may be helpful in assisting you to get closer to the problem of improving student engagement:

- What is the perception of teachers of the engagement level of their students?
- What is the perception of students as to their own engagement level?
- What is the perception of the students' parents as to the level of engagement, and what might the parent attribute that status to?
- What is the actual status of the engagement level of individual students?
- Why, as the leader, is the engagement status of individual learners not known?
- Why should student engagement status underpin the majority of what we do as student-centered leaders?
- Why are some of the students so engaged? Why are some students not engaged?

- What actions on the part of the teacher, student, or parent would reengage the learner?
- What is the teachers' knowledge level of the components of the Framework for Creating Passionate Learners?
- Specifically, what is the level of teacher knowledge in the skills, dispositions, internal conditions, and core beliefs of that framework?
- How visible is this teacher knowledge of the Framework for Creating Passionate Learners in daily instruction, feedback loops with students, and parent dialogue?
- What is the knowledge level on the same issue for building and district leaders?
- How are leaders modeling the knowledge?
- What are the leaders seen talking about?

Students today need schools that are vastly different from those in the past. The global demands placed on learners today and in the future require leaders who are truly student centered and who are willing to step out of what exists to lead in ways that matter to students. This change is going to be tougher than some may anticipate as the existing cultures, systems, structures, inertia, and people themselves each may serve as a significant hurdle.

This change must be transformative in nature, with high fidelity toward growth mindset, internal dialogue, self-determination, and culture within the Framework for Creating Passionate Learners. The landscape described and the student needs identified by the authors require a call to action similar in scope to many of the most significant educational changes of our time. Why the call to action, and why now? Public education needs action that results in a resurgence in stakeholder confidence, and the stakes are higher than ever in our careers.

With a spotlight on education from political forces and interest groups, our window to show improvement is short. If the education community does not rise to the occasion, someone else's version of change will happen in education that may not leverage student motivation or student learning. These changes will happen to the profession from outside sources, only further reducing confidence in the current system and people within the system. Educators must see this as our problem to solve and must see their collective contributions as essential. The changes needed in education are best facilitated by informed, leading educators who understand student engagement as central to learning.

The authors suggest a future of intentionally linking the Framework for Creating Passionate Learners to individual development plans for leaders. When we as leaders fully internalize the beliefs, skills, and dispositions outlined in the framework as applied to our own personal successes, limitations, and future, it is then where we have a greater understanding of student engagement issues. This understanding on the part of us as adults causes a far greater empathy for student challenges. When thinking about the leader to the learner impact and both being able to achieve significantly improved success, the framework and its use in schools takes on a deeper meaning.

Regarding excellence, educators have to do so much more than simply say we are about excellence. We must define excellence, expect it, and commit to it by supporting that charge with beliefs and strategies that will make a difference for students, strategies such as understanding and the full implementation of the Framework for Creating Passionate Learners. The education system of the future needs leaders with the knowledge, beliefs, and strategies that will get to very different results quickly by re-leveraging inspired students.

Our goal is that all students believe in their capacity to learn and their ability to develop skills to learn independently. Teachers that use language that allows students to understand mindset give learners autonomy for internal motivation. The language everyone uses can influence student mindset, including the self-talk the students give themselves. Culture is built together—everyone feels safe to take a risk, learn, and grow as a community. Giving students ownership in the learning process allows students to begin to see their capacity and thus could affect their own internal dialogues, mindsets, and self-determination. When each of these beliefs becomes common practice, it creates a culture where students can direct their own learning. When acting as interdependent beliefs, it is then that students have the capacity to develop their skills.

So, what will this leading and modeling look like? It will be a visible, new life throughout the leader's work. People notice leaders talking about issues real to students, real to what they are learning, to where and how they are learning, and possibly most importantly, to why they need to be learning. Leaders will have a mindfulness of student engagement influencing every facet of the organization. Leaders routinely support learners in thinking about their current levels of performance and their desired levels of performance. These leaders will touch on the very mindset, self-determination, and internal dialogue that matter so much to individual learners. Only through committed leaders can the support needed by staff and students create the conditions for an emerging culture of passionate learners.

We began this book examining anachronisms and arguing that education is ripe for creating new habits. The new habits are a resurgence on student engagement through the four beliefs.

1. Mindset: Engage students in tasks that they are motivated to accomplish because they spark students' curiosities and address their needs to develop and master new, relevant content and skills.

2. Internal Dialogue: Engage students in the habit of productive internal dialogue that is responsive to feedback as a catalyst to develop new skills and strategies that develop their capacity to be effective in any domain they choose.

3. Self-Determination: Engage students in opportunities to make choices about the work they do in a manner that builds ownership of their own learning and supports their needs for independence and autonomy.

4. Culture: Engage students in a culture of learning that is committed to finding solutions to problems that children see as meaningful and filled with purpose.

Understanding student status in behavioral, emotional, and cognitive engagement and being equipped with the knowledge and strategies to increase engagement are necessary in efforts aimed at improving student learning. Equipping teachers with the knowledge and skills to enhance student engagement creates a powerful lever to influence individual learners. In creating the conditions within individual students for them to have the ability to change perspective themselves, their attitudes and outlooks will alter their behaviors and choices forever. Educators need to see school through the students' eyes and then commit to the Framework for Creating Passionate Learners. This change will cause a shift in education: a shift that will make people someday reflect back and say that education that focuses on teaching and learning without a focus on student engagement—ah, an anachronism.

Appendix

Effort Tracker

3 I put in the time and effort and persisted in challenge.								
2 I put in the time and effort.								
1 I wasn't able to put in the time and effort this time.								
Assignment								

Every other week reflection: How has my investment in time and effort paying off in my growth in _____?

Resources

Abler, R. (2012, December 31). Deeper learning: A collaborative classroom is key [Web log message]. Retrieved from http://www.edutopia.org/blog/deeper-learning-collaboration-key-rebecca-alber

Ames, C., & Archer, J. (1988). Achievement goals in the classroom: Students' learning strategies and motivation processes. *Journal of Educational Psychology, 80*(3), 260–267.

Annual Report of the Superintendent of Common Schools of the State of New York. (2012). Charleston, SC: Nabu Press.

Ariely, D. (2013, April).What motivates us at work? The fascinating studies that gives insight. *TED Talks.* [Video]. Retrieved from http://blog.ted.com/2013/04/10/what-motivates-us-at-work-7-fascinating-studies-that-give-insights/

Assor, A. (2011). Autonomous moral motivation: Consequences, socializing antecedents and the unique role of integrated moral principles. In M. Mikulincer & P. R. Shaver (Eds.), *Social psychology of morality: Exploring the causes of good and evil.* Washington, DC: American Psychological Association.

Bandura, A. (1995). *Self-efficacy in changing societies.* New York: Cambridge University Press.

Barell, J. (2003). *Developing more curious minds.* Alexandria, VA: Association for Supervision and Curriculum Development.

Baumeister, R., & Tierney, J. (2011). *Willpower: Rediscovering the greatest human strength.* New York: Penguin Press.

Baseball Almanac. (2000–2014). Retrieved from http://www.baseball-almanac.com/hitting/histrk1.shtml

Barseghian, T. (2015, January 1). *How to foster grit, tenacity and perseverance: An educator's guide.* Retrieved from http://blogs.kqed.org/mindshift/2013/02/how-to-foster-grit-tenacity-and-perseverance-an-educators-guide/

Berns, R., & Erickson, P. (2001). *Contextual teaching and learning preparing students for the new economy.* Columbus, OH: National Dissemination Center for Career and Technical Education.

Black, A. E., & Deci, E. L. (2000). The effects of instructors' autonomy support and students' autonomous motivation on learning organic chemistry: A self-determination theory perspective. *Science Education, 84,* 740–756.

Blackwell, L., Trzesniewski, K., & Dweck, C. (2007). Implicit theories of intelligence predict achievement across an adolescent transition: A longitudinal study and an intervention. *Child Development, 78,* 246–263.

Blinco, P. M. A. (1993). Persistence and education: The formula for Japan's economic success. *Comparative Education, 29*(2), 171–183.

Bloom, B. (1956). *Taxonomy of educational objectives: The classification of educational goals.* New York: Longmans.

Blumberg, A., & Blumberg, P. (1985). *The school superintendent: Living with conflict.* New York: Teachers College, Columbia University.

Bocelli, A., Foster, D., Schwartz, A., Foster, G., & Skylark, N. (2006). Because we believe [Recorded by Andrea Bocelli]. On *Amore* [Album]. Peermusic Publishing, Spirit Music Group.

Boggiano, A. K., Flink, C., Shields, A., Seelbach, A., & Barrett, M. (1993). Use of techniques promoting students' self-determination: Effects on students' analytic problem-solving skills. *Motivation and Emotion, 17,* 319–336.

Brendgen, M., Wanner, B., Vitaro, F., Bukowski, W., & Tremblay, R. (2007). Verbal abuse by the teacher during childhood and academic, behavioral, and emotional adjustment in young adulthood. *Journal of Educational Psychology, 99*(1), 26–38.

Bruner, J. S. (1960). *The process of education.* Cambridge, MA: Harvard University Press.

Bruner, J. S. (1966). *Toward a theory of instruction.* Cambridge, MA: Belknap Press.

Bruner, J. (1996). *The culture of education.* Cambridge, MA: Harvard University Press.

Bryk, A., & Schneider, B. (2002). *Trust in schools: A core resource for improvement.* New York: Russell Sage Foundation.

Burnett, P. C. (1999). Children's self-talk and academic self-concepts. *Educational Psychology in Practice, 15,* 195–200.

Burton, W., Brueckner, L., & Barr, A. (1955). *Supervision, a social process* (3rd ed.). New York: Appleton-Century-Crofts.

Bush, G. (2000, July 10). Text: George W. Bush's speech to the NAACP. Retrieved from http://www.washingtonpost.com/wp-srv/onpolitics/elections/bushtext071000.htm

Carr, N. (2010). *The shallows: What the Internet is doing to our brains.* New York: W.W. Norton.

Catalano, R. F., Haggerty, K. P., Oesterle, S., Flemming, C. B., & Hawkins, J. D. (2004). The importance of binding to school for healthy development: Findings from the social development research group. *Journal of School Health, 74*(7), 252–261.

Chafouleas, S., Riley-Tillman, C., & Sugai, G. (2007). *School-based behavioral assessment: Informing intervention and instruction.* New York: Guilford.

Cherepinsky, V. (2011). Self-reflective grading: Getting students to learn from their mistakes. PRIMUS: *Journal of Problems, Resources, and Issues in Mathematics Undergraduate Studies, 21*(3), 294–301.

Chomsky, N., & Otero, C. (2003). *Chomsky on democracy & education.* New York: RoutledgeFalmer.

Christenson, S. L., Reschly, A. L., & Wylie, C. (Eds.). (2012). *Handbook of research on student engagement.* New York: Springer.

Costa, A. L., & Garmston, R. J. (2002). *Cognitive coaching: A foundation for renaissance schools.* Norwood, MA: Christopher-Gordon.

Costa, A. L., & Garmston, R. J. (2005). *Cognitive coaching foundation seminar* (6th ed.). Highlands Ranch, CO: Center for Cognitive Coaching.

Costa, A. L., & Kallick, B. (2008). *Learning and leading with habits of mind.* Alexandria, VA: Association for Supervision and Curriculum Development.

Costa, A. L., & Kallick, B. (2014). *Dispositions: Reframing teaching and learning.* Thousand Oaks, CA: Corwin.

Craven, R., Marsh, H., & Debus, R. (1991). Effects of internally focused feedback and attributional feedback on enhancement of academic self-concept. *Journal of Educational Psychology, 83,* 17–27.

Crooks, T. (1988). The impact of classroom evaluation practices on students. *Review of Educational Research, 58*(4), 438–481.

Csikszentmihalyi, M. (1990). *Flow: The psychology of optimal experience.* New York: HarperCollins.

Cubberley, E. (1922). *A brief history of education: A history of the practice and progress and organization of education.* Boston, MA: Houghton Mifflin.

Curtin, J. (1998). *Elvis: Unknown stories behind the legend.* Nashville, TN: Celebrity.

Dalai Lama Center. (2013, December 8). Can you teach compassion? [Web log message]. Retrieved from http://dalailamacenter.org/blog-post/can-you-teach-compassion

Danielson, C. (2007). *Enhancing professional practice: A framework for teaching* (2nd ed.). Alexandria, VA: Association for Supervision and Curriculum Development.

Dean, C., Hubbell, E., Pitler, H., & Stone, B. (2012). *Classroom instruction that works: Research-based strategies for increasing student achievement.* Alexandria, VA: Association for Supervision and Curriculum Development.

Deci, E., & Flaste, R. (1995). *Why we do what we do: Understanding self-motivation.* New York: Penguins.

Deci, E. L., & Ryan, R. M. (1991). A motivational approach to self: Integration in personality. In R. Dienstbier (Ed.), *Nebraska symposium on motivation: Perspectives on motivation* (Vol. 38, pp. 237–288). Lincoln: University of Nebraska Press.

Deci, E. L., & Ryan, R. M. (2000). The "what" and "why" of goal pursuits: Human needs and the self-determination of behavior. *Psychological Inquiry, 11*(4), 227–268.

Deming, W. (2000). *Out of the crisis.* Cambridge: Massachusetts Institute of Technology, Center for Advanced Engineering Study.

Dewey, J. (1916). *Democracy and education: Introduction to the philosophy of education.* New York: MacMillan.

Dewey, J. (1937). Lectures in educational philosophy (Unpublished stenographic typescript). Center for Dewey Studies, Southern Illinois University, Carbondale. Retrieved from http://docs.lib.purdue.edu/cgi/viewcontent.cgi?article=1467&context=eandc

Dickmann, M., & Stanford-Blair, N. (2009). *Mindful leadership: A brain-based framework* (2nd ed.). Thousand Oaks, CA: Corwin.

Doll, R., & Hill, A. (1950, September). Smoking and carcinoma of the lung. *British Medical Journal, 2*(4682), 739–748.

Dooly, M. (2008). *Telecollaborative language learning: A guidebook to moderating intercultural collaboration online.* Bern, Switzerland: Lang.

Downing, S. (2011). *On course: Strategies for creating success in college and in life* (6th ed.). Boston, MA: Wadsworth.

Drucker, P. (2002). *The effective executive.* New York: HarperCollins.

Duckworth, A. L., Peterson, C., Matthews, M. D., & Kelly, D. R. (2007). Grit: Perseverance and passion for long-term goals. *Journal of Personality and Social Psychology, 92,* 1087–1101.

Dunlosky, J., & Metcalf, J. (2009). *Metacognition.* Thousand Oaks, CA: Sage.

Dweck, C. S. (2000). *Self-theories: Their role in motivation, personality, and development.* New York: Psychology Press.

Dweck, C. S. (2006). *Mindset: The new psychology of success.* New York: Random House.

Dweck, C. S. (2010). Mind-sets and equitable education. *Principal Leadership, 10*(5), 26–29.

Dweck, C. (Performer). (2012). *Changing mindset webinar.* Retrieved from http://vts.inxpo.com/scripts/Server.nxp?LASCmd=AI:4;F:APIUTIL
S!51004&PageID=EB2B7AEA-758E-480E-BF41–6173545BA12A
&AffiliateData=EM-10.29

Dweck, C. S., & Elliot, E. S. (1983). Achievement motivation. In P. Mussen & E. M. Hetherington (Eds.), *Handbook of child psychology* (4th ed., pp. 643–691). New York: Wiley.

Dweck, C., Walton, G. M., & Cohen, G. L. (2011). *Academic tenacity: Mindsets and skills that promote long-term learning.* Paper presented at the Gates Foundation, Seattle, WA.

Elliot, A., & Dweck, C. (2005). *Handbook of competence and motivation.* New York: Guilford.

Elmore, R. F. (2006). What (so-called) low-performing schools can teach (so-called) high-performing schools. *Journal of Staff Development, 27*(2), 43–45.

Engel, S. (2013). The case for curiosity. *Educational Leadership, 70*(5), 36–40.

Epstein, J. L., & McPartland, J. M (1976). The concept and measurement of the quality of school life. *American Educational Research Journal, 13,* 15–30.

Ericsson, K. (2006). *The Cambridge handbook of expertise and expert performance.* Cambridge, UK: Cambridge University Press.

Ericsson, K., & Charness, N. (1994). Expert performance: Its structure and acquisition. *American Psychologist, 49*(8), 803–804.

Ericsson, K., Krampe, R., & Tesch-Römer, C. (1993). The role of deliberate practice in the acquisition of expert performance. *Psychological Review, 100*(3), 363–406.

Ericsson, K., Prietula, M., & Cokely, E. (2007, July 1). The making of an expert. Retrieved from https://hbr.org/2007/07/the-making-of-an-expert

Family of Vince Lombardi. (2010, January 1). Famous quotes by Vince Lombardi. Retrieved from http://www.vincelombardi.com/quotes.html

Farrington, C.A., Roderick, M., Allensworth, E., Nagaoka, J., Keyes, T. S., Johnson, D.W., & Beechum, N. O. (2012). *Teaching adolescents to become learners. The role of noncognitive factors in shaping school performance: A critical literature review.* Chicago, IL: University of Chicago Consortium on Chicago School Research.

Felix, A. (2000). *Andrea Bocelli: A celebration.* New York: St. Martin's Press.

Fine, J. (1997). Supervision for effective teaching in America 1910–1930. *The High School Journal, 80*(4), 40–54.

Finn, J. D. (1993). *School engagement and students at risk.* Washington, DC: National Center for Education Statistics.

Finn, J. D., & Zimmer, K. S. (2013). Student engagement: What is it? Why does it matter? In S. L. Christenson, A. L. Reschly, & C. Wylie (Eds.), *Handbook of research on student engagement* (pp. 97–132). New York: Springer.

Fredricks, J. A., Blumenfeld, P. C., & Paris, A. H. (2004). School engagement: Potential of the concept, state of the evidence. *Review of Educational Research, 74*(1), 59–109.

Friedman, T. (2005). *The world is flat: A brief history of the twenty-first century.* New York: Farrar, Straus and Giroux,

Frontier, A. (2007). *What is the relationship between student engagement and student achievement? A quantitative analysis of middle schools students' perceptions of their emotional, behavioral, and cognitive engagement as related to their performance on local and state measures of achievement.* (Doctoral dissertation). Retrieved from ProQuest. (ATT No. 3293073)

Frontier, T., & Rickabaugh, J. (2014). *Five levers to improve learning: How to prioritize for powerful results in your school.* Alexandria, VA: Association for Supervision and Curriculum Development.

Frontier, T., & Rickabaugh, J. (2015). Driving change. *Educational Leadership, 5*(72). Retrieved from http://www.ascd.org/publications/educational-leadership/feb15/v0172/num05/Driving-Change.aspx

Furrer, C., & Skinner, E. (2003). Sense of relatedness as a factor in children's academic engagement and performance. *Journal of Educational Psychology, 95*(1), 148–162.

Gabler, N. (2006). *Walt Disney: The triumph of the American imagination.* New York: Knopf, Borzoi.

Gage, N. L., & Berliner, D. C. (1998). *Educational psychology.* Boston, MA: Houghton Mifflin.

Gallup. (2014, October 1). Gallup student poll. Retrieved from file:///Users/kim.brown/Downloads/Gallup Student Poll 2014 U.S. Overall Report (1).pdf

Gardner, H. (1983). Frames of mind: The theory of multiple intelligences. New York: Basic Books.

Gentry, M., Gable, R. K., & Rizza, M. G. (2002). Students' perceptions of classroom activities: Are there grade-level and gender differences? *Journal of Educational Psychology, 94*(3), 539–544.

Gibbons, M. (2014). *Motivating students and teaching them to motivate themselves.* Retrieved from http://selfdirectedlearning.com/teaching-self-directed-learning-tools/articles/empowering-students.html

Gladwell, M. (2008). *Outliers: The story of success.* New York: Little, Brown.

Glasser, W. (1998). *Choice theory: A new psychology of personal freedom.* New York: HarperCollins.

Gould, S. (1981). *The mismeasure of man.* New York: W.W. Norton.

Grant, H., & Dweck, C. (2003). Clarifying achievement goals and their impact. *Journal of Personality and Social Psychology, 85*(3), 541–553.

Graves, D. (2006). *A sea of faces: The importance of knowing your students.* Portsmouth, NH: Heinemann.

Hacker, J., Dunlosky, J., & Graesser, A. (2009). *Handbook of metacognitions in education.* New York: Routledge.

Hall, P., & Simeral, A. (2008). *Building teachers' capacity for success: A collaborative approach for coaches and school leaders.* Alexandria, VA: Association for Supervision and Curriculum Development.

Harvey, S., & Goudvis, A. (2007). *Strategies that work: Teaching comprehension for understanding and engagement.* Portland, ME: Stenhouse.

Hattie, J. (2009). *Visible learning: A synthesis of over 800 meta-analyses relating to achievement.* New York: Routledge.

Hattie, J. (2012). *Visible learning for teachers: Maximizing impact on learning.* London: Routledge.

Hattie, J., & Timperley, H. (2007). The power of feedback. *Review of Educational Research, 77,* 81–112.

Hatzigeorgiadis, A., Zourbanos, N., Mpoumpaki, S., & Theodorakis, Y. (2008). Mechanisms underlying the self-talk–performance relationship: The effects of motivational self-talk on self-confidence and anxiety. *Psychology of Sport and Exercise, 10,* 186–192.

Henderson, N. (2013). Havens of resilience. *Educational Leadership, 71*(1), 23–27.

Jacobs, J. E., Lanza, S., Osgood, W. D., Eccles, J. S., & Wigfield, A. (2002). Changes in children's self-competence and values: Gender and domain differences across grades one through twelve. *Child Development, 73*(2), 509–528.

Jang, H., Reeve, J., & Deci, E. L. (2010). Engaging students in learning activities: It is not autonomy support or structure, but autonomy support and structure. *Journal of Educational Psychology, 102,* 588–600.

Johnson-Smith, K. (2005). *Creating a safe space for students to take academic risks.* Learn North Carolina. Retrieved from http://www.learnnc.org/lp/editions/firstyear/258

Johnston, P. H. (2004). *Choice words: How our language affects children's language.* Portland, ME: Stenhouse.

Johnston, P. H. (2012). *Opening minds: Using language to change lives.* Portland, ME: Stenhouse.

Johnston, P. H., Woodside-Jiron, H., & Day, J. (2001). Teaching and learning literate epistemologies. *Journal of Educational Psychology, 93*(1), 223–233. doi: 10.1037/002200663.93.1.223

Kaplan, A., Gheen, M., & Midgley, C. (2002). Classroom goal structure and student disruptive behaviour. *British Journal of Educational Psychology, 72*(6), 191–211.

Katz, L. (1993). Dispositions: Definitions and implications for early childhood practices. *ERIC Clearinghouse on Elementary and Early Childhood Education,* 1–55.

Katz, I., & Assor, A. (2007). When choice motivates and when it does not. *Educational Psychology Review, 19,* 429–442.

Kelley, T., & Littman, J. (2001). *The art of innovation: Lessons in creativity from IDEO, America's leading design firm.* New York: Crown Business.

Klem, A., & Connell, J. (2004). Relationships matter: Linking teacher support to student engagement and achievement. *Journal of School Health, 74*(7), 262–273.

Koestner, R., Ryan, R. M., Bernieri, F., & Holt, K. (1984). Setting limits on children's behavior: The differential effects of controlling versus informational styles on intrinsic motivation and creativity. *Journal of Personality, 52,* 233–248.

Kohn, A. (1999). *Punished by rewards: The trouble with gold stars, incentive plans, A's, praise, and other bribes.* Boston, MA: Houghton Mifflin.

Kohn, A. (2004, November). Challenging students and how to have more of them. *Phi Delta Kappan.* Retrieved from http://www.alfiekohn .org/teaching/challenging.htm

Kohn, A. (2006). *The homework myth: Why our kids get too much of a bad thing.* Cambridge, MA: Da Capo Life Long.

Kolb, S., & Stevens-Griffith, A. (2009). I'll repeat myself again?! Empowering students through assertive communication strategies. *Teaching Exceptional Children, 41*(3), 32–36.

Koutstaal, W. (2012). *The agile mind.* New York: Oxford University Press.

Lacy, J. (2009). 10 tips to connect with your child [Web log message]. Retrieved from http://www.pbs.org/thisemotionallife/blogs/10-tips-connect-your-child

Lan, W. (2005). Self-monitoring and its relationship with educational level and task importance. *Educational Psychology, 25,* 109–127.

Langford, D. P., & Cleary, B. A. (1995). *Orchestrating learning with quality.* Milwaukee, WI: ASQC Quality Press.

Lashinsky, A. (2012, January 19). Larry Page: Google should be like a family. *Fortune.* Retrieved from http://fortune.com/2012/01/19/ larry-page-google-should-be-like-a-family/

Licht, B. G., & Dweck, C. S. (1984). Determinants of academic achievement: The interaction of children's achievement orientations with skill area. *Developmental Psychology, 20,* 628–636.

Loftin, R. L., Gibb, A. C., & Skiba, R. (2005). Using self-monitoring strategies to address behavior and academic issues. *Impact, 18*(2). Retrieved from https://ici.umn.edu/products/impact/182/over6 .html

Marks, H. M. (2000). Student engagement in instructional activity: Patterns in the elementary, middle, and high school years. *American Educational Research Journal, 37,* 153–184.

Marsh, H. W. (1989). Age and sex effects in multiple dimensions of self-concept: Preadolescence to early adulthood. *Journal of Educational Psychology, 81,* 417–430.

Martin, S. (2014). "Changing the Narrative: Evidence. Action. Impact." Visible Learning Plus International Conference, Park Hyatt Aviara Resort, San Diego, CA. 18 July 2014. Lecture.

Marzano, R. (2007). *The art and science of teaching: A comprehensive framework for effective instruction.* Alexandria, VA: Association for Supervision and Curriculum Development.

Marzano, R. J., Pickering, D. J., & Pollock, J. E. (2001). *Classroom instruction that works: Research-based strategies for increasing student achievement.* Alexandria, VA: Association for Supervision and Curriculum Development.

Maslow, A. H. (1943). A theory of human motivation. *Psychological Review, 50*(4), 370–96. Retrieved from http://psychclassics.yorku .ca/Maslow/motivation.htm

Merton, R. (1949). *Social theory and social structure: Toward the codification of theory and research.* Chicago: The Free Press of Glencoe Illinois.

National Center for Education Statistics. (2014, January 1). Fast facts. Retrieved from http://nces.ed.gov/fastfacts/display.asp?id=16

National Research Council and the Institute of Medicine. (2004). *Engaging schools: Fostering high school students' motivation to learn.* Washington, DC: National Academy Press.

Newmann, F. M. (Ed.). (1992). *Student engagement and achievement in American secondary schools.* New York: Teachers College Press.

Obama, B. (2009, September 8). Prepared remarks of President Barack Obama: Back to school event. Retrieved from http://www.white house.gov/MediaResources/PreparedSchoolRemarks/

Pedersen, S., & Williams, D. (2004). A comparison of assessment practices and their effects on learning and motivation in a student-centered learning environment. *Journal of Educational Multimedia and Hypermedia, 13*(3), 283–306.

Perkins-Gough, D. (2013). The significance of grit: A conversation with Angela Lee Duckworth. *Educational Leadership, 71*(1), 14–20.

Piaget, J. (1923). *The language and thought of the child.* London: Routledge & Paul.

Piaget, J. (1947). *The psychology of intelligence.* London: Routledge & Paul.

Pianta, R. C., Hamre, B. K., & Allen, J. P. (2011). Teacher–student relationships and engagement: Conceptualizing, measuring, and improving the capacity of classroom interactions. In S. L. Christenson, A. L. Reschly, & C. Wylie (Eds.), *Handbook research on student engagement.* New York: Springer.

Pilcher, J., & Largue, R. (2009). *How to lead teachers to become great: It's all about student learning.* Gulf Breeze, FL: Fire Starter.

Pink, D. H. (2009). *Drive: The surprising truth about what motivates us.* New York: Riverhead.

Popham, W. J. (2008). *Transformative assessment.* Alexandria, VA: Association for Supervision and Curriculum Development.

Prast, H., & Viegut, D. (2015). *Community-based learning: Awakening the mission of public schools.* Thousand Oaks, CA: Corwin.

Quaglia, R. J., & Corso, M. J. (2014). *Student voice: The instrument of change.* Thousand Oaks: CA: Corwin.

Rafanelli, S. (2012, November 6). Why cheat? More importantly, why not? Retrieved from http://www.challengesuccess.org/

Reeve, J. (2006). Teachers as facilitators: What autonomy-supportive teachers do and why their students benefit. *The Elementary School Journal, 106*, 225–236.

Reeve, J., Bolt, E., & Cai, Y. (1999). Autonomy-supportive teachers: How they teach and motivate students. *Journal of Educational Psychology, 91*(3), 537–548.

Reeve, J., Jang, H., Carrell, D., Barch, J., & Jeon, S. (2004). Enhancing students' engagement by increasing teachers' autonomy support. *Motivation and Emotion, 28*, 147–169.

Renzulli, J. S. (2010). *Freedom to teach.* Mansfield Center, CT: Creative Learning.

Reschly, A. L., & Christenson, S.L. (2013). Jingle, jangle and conceptual haziness: Evolution and future direction on engagement construct. In S. L. Christenson, A. L. Reschly, & C. Wylie (Eds.), *Handbook of research on student engagement* (pp. 3–20). New York: Springer.

Rickabaugh, J. (2011, May 5). Interview by K. Cooke [Lecture]. Superintendency, Cardinal Stritch University.

Romanowski, M. H. (2004, Summer). Student obsession with grades and achievement. *Kappa Delta Pi Record, 40*(4), 149–151.

Roth, G., Assor, A., Niemiec, P. C., Ryan, R. M., & Deci, E. L. (2009). The negative consequences of parental conditional regard: A comparison of positive conditional regard, negative conditional regard, and autonomy support as parenting strategies. *Developmental Psychology, 4*, 1119–1142.

Rotter, J. B., Chance, J. E., & Phares, E. J. (1972). *Applications of a social learning theory of personality.* New York: Holt, Rinehart & Winston.

Russell, B. (1939). Education for democracy. *Addresses and Proceedings of the National Education Association, 77*. (See also Philosophy for laymen. [1950]. In *Unpopular Essays.* London: George Allen and Unwin.)

Russell, J., & Cohn, R. (2012). *Is Google making us stupid?* Retrieved from http://books.google.com/books/about/Is_Google_Making_Us_Stupid.html?id=KlZwMAEACAAJ

Ryan, A. M., Gheen, M. H., & Midgley, C. (1998). Why do some students avoid asking for help? An examination of the interplay among students academic efficacy, teachers social-emotional role, and the classroom goal structure. *Journal of Educational Psychology, 90*, 528–535.

Ryan, R., & Deci, E. (2000). Self-determination theory and the facilitation of intrinsic motivation, social development, and well-being. *American Psychology, 55*, 68–78.

Sagor, R. (1996). Building resiliency in students. *Educational Leadership,* 54(1), 38–43. Retrieved from http://www.ascd.org/publications/ educational-leadership/sept96/v0154/num01/Building-Resi liency-in-Students.aspx

Saphier, J., Haley-Speca, M., & Gower, R. (2008). *The skillful teacher: Building your teaching skills* (6th ed.). Acton, MA: Research for Better Teaching.

Scherer, M. (Ed.). (2005). Valuing children. *Educational Leadership, 63*(1), 7.

Schlechty, P. (1997). *Inventing better schools: An action plan for educational reform.* San Francisco, CA: Jossey-Bass.

Schlechty, P. (2002). *Working on the work: An action plan for teachers, principals, and superintendents.* San Francisco, CA: Jossey-Bass.

Schlechty, P.C. (2011). *Engaging students: The next level of working on the work.* San Francisco, CA: Jossey-Bass.

Schunk, D. H. (2009, December 21). Goal setting [Web log message]. Retrieved from http://www.education.com/reference/article/goal-setting/

Schunk, D. H., & Mullen, C.A. (2012). Self-efficacy as an engaged learner. In S. L. Christenson, A. L. Reschly, & C. Wylie (Eds.), *Handbook of research on student engagement* (pp. 219–235). New York: Springer.

Schunk, D. H., & Rice, J. M. (1991). Learning goals and progress feedback during reading comprehension instruction. *Journal of Reading Behavior, 23,* 351–364.

Scriven, M., & Paul, R. (1987, Summer). *Critical thinking as defined by the National Council for Excellence in Critical Thinking.* Retrieved from https://www.criticalthinking.org/pages/defining-critical-think ing/766

Self-Brown, S., & Matthews, II, S. (2003). Effects of classroom structure on student achievement goal. *The Journal of Educational Research, 97*(2), 106–111.

Seligman, M., Revich, K., M.A., Jaycox, L., & Gilham, J. (2007). *An optimistic child: A proven program to safeguard children against depression and build lifelong resilience.* New York: Houghton Mifflin.

Shapira, Z. (1976). Expectancy determinants of intrinsically motivated behavior. *Journal of Personality and Social Psychology, 34,* 1235–1244.

Shepard, L. A. (2000). The role of assessment in a learning culture. *Educational Researcher, 29*(7), 4–14.

Shernoff, D., Csikszentmihalyi, M., Schneider, B., & Shernoff, E. (2003). Student engagement in high school classrooms from the perspective of flow theory. *School Psychology Quarterly, 18*(2), 158–176.

Skinner, E., & Belmont, M. (1993). Motivation in the classroom: Reciprocal effects of teacher behavior and student engagement across the school year. *Journal of Educational Psychology, 85*(4), 571.

Smith, K. A., Sheppard, S. D., Johnson D. W., & Johnson, R. T. (2005). Pedagogies of engagement: Classroom-based practices. *Journal of Engineering Education, 94*(1), 87–102.

Spring, J. (2011). *American education* (15th ed.). New York: McGraw-Hill.

Sternberg, R. J. (2005). Intelligence, competence, and expertise. In A. J. Elliot & C. S. Dweck (Eds.), *Handbook of competence and motivation* (pp. 15–30). New York: Guilford.

Stevenson, H. W., & Stigler, J. W. (1992). *The learning gap: Why our schools are failing and what we can learn from Japanese and Chinese education.* New York: Summit Books.

Stiggins, R. (2001). *Student-involved classroom assessment* (3rd ed.). Upper Saddle River, NJ: Merrill Prentice Hall.

Studer, Q. (2003). *Hardwiring excellence.* Gulf Breeze, FL: Fire Starter.

Taylor, F. (1911). *The principles of scientific management.* New York: Harper and Brothers.

U.S. Department of Education. (2013, January 1). Homeroom. In *NCES common core of data state dropout and completion data file, school year 2009–10, version 1a.* National Center for Education Statistics, Common Core of Data. Retrieved from http://www.ed.gov/blog/2013/01/high-school-graduation-rate-at-highest-level-in-three-decades/

Vallerand, R. J., Fortier, M. S., & Guay, F. (1997). Self-determination and persistence in a real-life setting: Toward a motivational model of high school dropout. *Journal of Personality and Social Psychology, 72,* 1161–1176.

Vezzali, L., Stathi, S., Giovannini, D., Capozza, D., & Trifiletti, E. (2014). The greatest magic of Harry Potter: Reducing prejudice. *Journal of Applied Psychology.* doi: 10.1111/jasp.12279

Vygotsky, L. S. (1978). *Mind in society: The development of the higher psychological processes.* Cambridge, MA: Harvard University Press.

Vygotsky, L. S. (1989). Concrete human psychology. *Soviet Psychology, 27*(2), 53–77.

Webb, N. (1997). *Criteria for alignment of expectations and assessments in mathematics and science education.* Madison, WI: National Institute for Science Education.

Whimbey, A. (1980, April). Students can learn to be better problem solvers. *Educational Leadership, 559–565.* Retrieved from http://www.ascd.org/ascd/pdf/journals/ed_lead/el_198004_whimbey.pdf

Wielsen, N. (2014, January 14). Teaching persistence: How to build student stamina [Web log message]. Retrieved from http://www.scilearn.com/blog/teaching-persistence-how-to-build-student-stamina

Willingham, D. T. (2007). Can critical thinking be taught? *American Educator, Summer,* 8–19.

Willingham, D. (2011, Summer). Can teachers increase students' self-control. *American Educator, 22*–27. Retrieved from http://www.aft.org//sites/default/files/periodicals/Willingham_3.pdf

Willms, J. D. (2003). *Student engagement at school: A sense of belonging and participation.* Paris, France: Organization for Economic Co-operation and Development.

Winkler, M. (2013). What makes a hero? *TED-ed.* [Video]. Retrieved from http://ed.ted.com/lessons/what-makes-a-hero-matthew-winkler

Wynder, E., & Graham, E. (1950). Tobacco smoking as a possible etiologic factor in bronchiogenic carcinoma: A study of six hundred and eighty-four proved cases. *JAMA: The Journal of the American Medical Association, 253*(20), 2986–2994.

Yazzie-Mintz, E. (2006). *Voices of students on engagement: A report on the 2006 high school survey of student engagement.* Bloomington: Center for Evaluation & Education Policy, Indiana University.

Yeager, D., Purdie-Vaughns, V., Garcia, J., Apfel, N., Brzustoski, P., . . . Master, A. (2013). Breaking the cycle of mistrust: Wise interventions to provide critical feedback across the racial divide. *Journal of Experimental Psychology: General,* 1–21. doi: 10.1037/a0033906

Zourbanos, N., Hatzigeorgiadis, A., Tsiakaras, N., Chroni, S., & Theodorakis, Y. (2010). A multimethod examination of the relationship between coaching behavior and athletes' inherent self-talk. *Journal of Sport and Exercise Psychology, 32,* 764–785.

Zumbrunn, S., Tadlock, J., & Roberts, E. (2011, October 1). Encouraging self-regulated learning in the classroom: A review of the literature. Retrieved from http://www.self-regulation.ca/download/pdf_docu ments/Self%20Regulated%20Learning.pdf

Index

A SAGE Company

CORWIN HAS ONE MISSION: to enhance education through intentional professional learning.

We build long-term relationships with our authors, educators, clients, and associations who partner with us to develop and continuously improve the best evidence-based practices that establish and support lifelong learning.